VIVE LE SPORT!

Printed by S.S.W. Ltd.
19/21 Great Portland St, London W1.

I.S.B.N. 0 9506693 0X

VIVE LE SPORT!

by

CHRISTOPHER CURTIS

illustrated by

JOHN TICKNER

**(with some less artistic
contributions by the Author)**

Christopher Curtis Publications
Borrowdale House,
Carthorpe,
Bedale,
North Yorkshire

ACKNOWLEDGEMENTS

I am deeply indebted to the Editor of Shooting Times & Country Magazine, in which the majority of the articles, verses and snippets in this book first appeared, and also to the Editor of Horse & Hound for their permission to reprint.

My thanks also to John Tickner whose pen has delighted so many country sportsmen for many years, both with his writings and his artistry and who illustrated my first attempt at humour many years ago.

I must also acknowledge with thanks the many huntsmen, shoot organisers and riparian owners whose hospitality I am probably abusing by publishing this book. Likewise, appreciation is due to those who, on their own account, or jointly with their animals, have provided me with my material.

To the British Field Sports Society I am also grateful, for it was while working on its behalf that I gained experience of many country sports. Also, it is that Society, the Wildfowlers' Association of Great Britain and Ireland, together with other organisations, which have helped preserve our country sports and make it possible for us still to enjoy ourselves in what remains of our countryside.

INTRODUCTION

My early involvement with country sports could hardly be described as a great success and it seemed unlikely, to say the least, that they would provide me with as much fun as they have in later years.

Apart from the frequent attendance of doctors (after falls from ponies I could not control), my clearest recollections of learning to ride centre round a large spinster lady, to whom my parents had entrusted my tuition and whose loud, frequent and publicly expressed opinions of my ability probably gave me the idea that shooting might be a more congenial sport. The subsequent change of allegiance thus induced did not get away to a happy start when the very first two shots I ever fired missed my toes by about three inches. They also removed two divots from my uncle's tennis court and caused his already ruddy complexion — and his language — to turn a deep purple. As to fishing, I discarded that at an early age when I discovered, after long hours of eager expectancy, the only thing my bent pin ever gathered was rust.

These early disappointments and a number of later mishaps notwithstanding, I have since derived an enormous amount of pleasure from participation in most branches of country sport. So that we can enjoy country sports, those who organise them put in many hours, days and weeks of very hard work, but this book does not touch on such weighty matters. It is intended to reflect the fun of our traditional sports — hence its title — Vive le Sport!

Christopher Curtis.

CONTENTS

TO BOOT AND TO SADDLE

Circumstances combined, over a period of some twenty years, to keep me well away from horses. First, the design of fighter aircraft is such as not to allow space for the carriage of all the accoutrements required for riding, let alone the transport of a horse. Then, at a time when I might have ventured back into the saddle, an orthopaedic surgeon found it necessary to remove a bit of my back and I deemed it inadvisable to impose any additional strain on that part of my anatomy.

My employment by the British Field Sports Society changed all that. For some reason everyone took it for granted that someone in my position must automatically be a devil of a chap to hounds and I found myself turning down an embarrassing number of invitations to be a participant in a day's sport. Eventually, an invitation from my Chairman to stay for the weekend and to hunt was one which I felt I could not refuse – largely, I admit, because I did not wish to be thought guilty of cowardice; this, to a practising (but so far undetected) coward is important.

The day of the hunt was bright and sunny but the thought of the approaching Meet and all that might ensue hung like a black cloud on my mental horizon. On arrival at the Meet my horse was ready and waiting – and what a horse it was! My host was a man who is – how shall I put it – generously built and the mount he had provided for me looked large enough quite easily to carry both of us. A mild attack of vertigo passed off soon after I was hoisted aboard and it was with some relief that I found myself still in the saddle when we moved off.

1

Twenty years away from horses had erased the philology of the horse world from my memory, and when my host's son remarked of my horse in a friendly way, "Watch out, he hangs on a bit," I was none the wiser. While still pondering on the meaning of this possibly vital piece of information, I suddenly underwent the sort of acceleration normally only experienced by the pilots of supersonic aircraft when they cut in the afterburners. I slid rapidly towards the end of the horse from which the tail hangs and was only saved from falling off altogether by the reins. Clambering back into a more dignified position I endeavoured to reduce the speed at which my horse and of necessity I, too, were travelling. It immediately became apparent what 'hangs on a bit' meant. Nothing on earth would slow the animal down. In the course of the next 20 minutes and only barely remaining within Wiltshire's boundaries, we covered an enormous amount of ground at a very considerable speed. While unable to reduce my horse's forward velocity in any way, I did discover that maximum pressure on one rein had a marginal effect on the direction he took and it was thus that I eventually managed to rejoin the hunt at a point where they had checked.

This check served only to allow my mount to retrieve his breath and, when hounds set off in pursuit of their fox once again, he was electrified into an instant gallop. It was then, to my utter dismay, I discovered we were in a field entirely surrounded by a six-strand barbed wire fence. Employing the technique I had earlier found to have some effect, I persuaded him to encircle the field. Having broken the standing start lap record for this particular meadow by a large margin we arrived at the only gate to find it still blocked by some 40 members of the field waiting to get through. Hardly hesitating, my valiant steed veered slightly to one side and made straight for the fence. I did my best but, realising some six yards short of the wire that there was no stopping him, I closed my eyes and gave him his head. In jumping the fence he rose to a considerable height but it was nevertheless a lot lower than the altitude which I attained. Fortunately I retained my forward velocity and the parabola I described terminated back in the saddle when we reached the other side of this horrifying fence. On we galloped until alongside me came an immaculately clad rider. "Tell me," he enquired politely, "Do you always jump wire in your country, sir?" But by now my face was fixed in a rigid grimace, caused equally by strain and terror and I was quite unable to answer.

My next experience in the hunting field took place in Yorkshire after I had received an assurance that my proposed mount had no propensity for jumping wire. This was a hunt of a very different character. It seemed that no sooner had we left the Meet than hounds were in full cry down a steep hillside, up another one and finally up onto the high ground where we galloped and jumped, galloped and jumped. On the basis that my horse knew more about jumping than I did – a reasonable assumption in the circumstances – I let him do what he thought best. This worked very well for a time but, before long, muscles that had become atrophied through years of non-use began to ache and my limbs grew more and more tired. Sooner or later something unpleasant was bound to happen. It turned out to be sooner. The fox we were pursuing suddenly decided to make a sharp turn to the left. He was followed by the hounds, the huntsman, the field and my horse, but not, unfortunately, by me. The moment my horse chose to execute the turn came just as he touched down on the other side of a fence and, following my usual procedure, I had not at this point returned to the saddle. I therefore continued on in a straight line. While airborne I became inverted and then gradually lost altitude until my head came in contact with the ground. I thus ploughed a neat head-shaped furrow in an otherwise level Yorkshire field and converted my once immaculate office bowler into a muddy homburg.

An illustrious pack, noted equally for the quality of the sport it offered and for the standard of sartorial perfection of those who followed it, provided the venue for my next day in the saddle. My recently purchased hunting clothes, topped by the aforementioned and restored bowler hat, had by now taken on an air of quaint if battered respectability. The effect was slightly marred by the cut that had been made in the top of my boot to allow for a swollen leg – the result of an earlier mishap. Initially, the gap was small but gradually it enlarged, allowing a considerable amount of my wife's nylon stocking which I was wearing to become exposed to view. It says much for the restraint of those present that no one commented on the sudden appearance in their midst of a swollen, hairy, nylon-clad leg. Most of the hazards that day turned out to be walls. This was a sad circumstance for me as I had earlier been warned that my mount had a tendency to investigate the other side of walls before actually jumping them. This meant that I was subjected to a fierce deceleration just short of each wall which inevitably resulted in my being propelled forward to a position immediately behind the horse's ears. However, the subsequent jump had the effect of returning me to a more central position. A refusal at one stage (caused by my own apprehension rather than the horse's) interrupted the sequence and prevented the restoration of the status quo. My subsequent progress, balanced on what I now know are referred to as the withers, was less than dignified.

At least until now I had not made an utter fool of myself and had fallen off under reasonably honourable conditions, but Nemesis was at hand. The next Meet I attended was a lawn meet, a truly social gathering with dutch courage being handed round in the form of stirrup cups. Suddenly my horse lay down. To retain one's dignity with a foot trapped under a horse, bowler hat askew and a glass in one hand is, I now know, an impossibility. A ring of human and equine faces looked down upon me with expressions of amazement and sympathy. Remounted, I felt happier again after a bit of hunting and when I had successfully negotiated several obstacles of varying heights. Some time later, relaxed and trotting along the road to a new covert, we rounded a corner. By the roadside lay a lump of machinery covered with a sheet of cellophane and it was as I passed it that the covering, caught by a gust of wind, blew up in my horse's face. He shied, reared up and slipped, any one of which would have sufficed to remove me from the saddle. The combination of all three had the effect of shooting me through the air, culminating in a three-point landing on a very hard piece of tarmac.

Fortuitously, my ankle, hip and elbow had made contact with the forecourt of an inn and I found myself looking up into the startled face of a man quaffing a pint of beer. Thrusting the reins into his free hand, I made my way shakily in through the door marked "Saloon". When I rejoined the hunt some time later, I was asked by a kindly lady if I was all right, with the added comment, "I hope you had a pint of beer while you were there." I nodded and smiled happily back at her, remembering the three large brandies I had downed during my enforced absence from the chase and which had, partially, restored my nerve.

In spite of such a poor start, I persevered and now have my own horse. The intervals between falls are still depressingly short and increasing age and weight ensure that I gravitate earthwards with a great deal more force than did Newton's apple. I have, however, the greatest faith in the continued ability of the medical profession to keep me roadworthy — at least for a few more seasons.

A GOOD TENPENNYWORTH

It is not every day that one gets stabbed, comes under heavy machine-gun fire and has to beg a lift back from hunting in a passing lorry, so I think it is worth recording the facts. Lest I might be accused of garnishing the tale with untruthful spice, I should mention that there are a number of reliable witnesses to the whole affair.

Although the events of which I write occurred in late January, in order to put the whole affair in its proper perspective, it is first necessary to return to the middle of the previous summer and, in particular, to the day when the local branch of the Riding for the Disabled Association held their annual Fête. Now a fête, if not actually worse than death, certainly registers high on my list of least favourite forms of entertainment. Gina, however, enjoys them and duly represented the family on this occasion, returning thence with, among other purchases, the most beautiful pair of breeches. Lovat green in colour, with a delicate blue cross check, made of real quality cloth and apparently unworn they were. On this useful garment Gina had expended the princely sum of ten pence.

The reason for the knock-down price only became obvious when I tried them on, to discover that, although they fitted perfectly, the breeches were constructed after the fashion of yesteryear with absolutely enormous "wings". My appearance in them caused such mirth that some minutes passed before the family recovered sufficiently to pass a unanimous vote against their ever being worn by me in public. They therefore lay unused in a drawer for some months before the coincidence of a bye-day and my other breeches not having recovered from a series of muddy days gave me the chance to don them.

Bearing in mind the earlier threat by one of our Joint Masters to send me home should I dare to appear in the breeches, I took care to mount out of sight and most of the offending cloth was hidden beneath the flaps of my jacket by the time I hove in sight. Not appreciating that we were to be entertained at the Meet, I had earlier downed a couple of quick ones, an action I was almost immediately to regret when approached by an aged retainer with a vast tumbler about one third full of neat whisky. Before I could accept it, however, he extracted from under his arm a bottle of the same stuff, the contents of which he sloshed into the glass until it was full almost to the brim.

Even in spite of this gargantuan spiritual measure, all might have been well had not James, who had lulled me into a false sense of security by behaving impeccably until then, chosen the moment when hounds moved off to put in a quick one. This unscheduled movement coincided with my attempting to drain the glass, causing the contents to shoot to the back of my throat, thereby inducing a choking fit and a sharpish performance of the elephant trick. Endeavouring to cover this unedifying spectacle with a hand, I inadvertently disconnected my stock pin, the point of which penetrated my hand to some depth and released a gush of blood to join the whisky pouring out of my nose and the tears streaming from my eyes.

I had recovered enough by the time we climbed up to the first draw to admire the superb views of the dale in which we met, renowned alike for its picturesque landscape and its cheese. Recovered enough, too, to notice that I was not the only beneficiary of our hostess's liberal hospitality, for there was an air of unrestrained jollity among the field. Perhaps it was this that decided the Field Master to lead us on a warm-up canter alongside the covert. Should this seem in no way remarkable, I must explain that the wood is hung on a steep hillside and topped by a cliff at the edge of which runs a track. The track is not only narrow, winding and slippery, but liberally dotted with trees, the over-hanging branches of which force the rider to duck frequently or risk being swept over the cliff. We were all warm by the time we reached the end and even warmer when, the draw being blank, we did an about turn and reversed the process.

Hounds were quickly away from the next covert and, after a short scamper, we pulled up beside a fir wood in which our quarry sought temporary refuge. Here I was sent to a vantage point from which I soon observed some caps aloft by the roadside and heard excited holloas. Deeming a fox to be afoot and having identified the bared heads as belonging to normally reliable fellows, I had added the odd "Whooi!" to the general din before discovering, to my horror, that Charles had been seen in and not leaving covert. Luckily, hounds disregarded me and left the wood by another exit in close pursuit, so my misdemeanour passed unnoticed — almost. Unusually for me I had surmounted a gate on the way, and, by the time I had renegotiated this object, I was well behind.

Delays caused by first one and then another Master becoming entangled in wire gave me the chance to make good the deficit and I was catching up nicely as our fox took us over a number of walled grass fields and set his mask for the moors. Whether he was colour-blind and failed to notice the red flags or preferred the risk of a chance bullet to the more obviously pressing danger behind him, I do not know. He kept straight on into the sound of heavy firing which became ominously loud as we too advanced on to the moor. Firing ceased ("Thank God, they're friendly!" I thought) at about the same time that a diminution in scent slowed our progress, thus giving the Range Officer a chance to take a hand in the proceedings. Although too far away to hear his words of greeting, it was obvious.that we were not altogether welcome. While the terms of the treaty were being worked out and feeling the need (it was a chilly day) to dismount, I took advantage of a wall. That the wall was not high enough I did not realise until a number of extremely unfunny remarks about my breeches were made when I rejoined the field, by now beating a dignified retreat under a white flag.

Out on the road, it was a minute or two before I noticed that James, instead of his customary clip-clop, clip-clop, was going phut-clop, phut-clop. From this I was able correctly to deduce that his front shoes were embedded somewhere among the spent bullets. Once again I had to dismount to a chorus of ribald comments, acutely conscious that my slightly undersized ratcatcher jacket was doing little to conceal the voluminous olde worlde appearance of my nether garment. Gina took James, I took her whip and walked up to the main road for a lift back to the trailer with one of the car followers. Sadly I arrived in time to see the last of the cars, filled to overflowing with others on the same mission, disappearing down the road.

So there I was, looking like a First World War Cavalry Officer whose horse had been shot from under him (not so far from the truth as it happened) and waiting for a passing limber to take him back to the rear lines. The limber duly appeared in the shape of a huge lorry, which, to my surprise and with a hissing of airbrakes, pulled up in response to my hopefully extended thumb. Brave fellow that driver. Had it been me in his place, driving through the wintry gloom of a lonely moor and seeing a strangely attired man wearing kinky boots, two whips in one hand, making odd gestures with the other and a hopeful smile on his face, I would not have stopped. I would have put my foot hard down and dialled 999 at the first opportunity.

My benefactor dropped me at the entrance to a quarry a few miles down the road, opposite which, amazingly, was yet another lorry driver willing to accept me as a passenger. This second Samaritan deposited me in the market square of Leyburn with still a mile and a half to go. Happily, my exposure to the gaze of an astonished general public was shortlived. I had barely reached the outskirts of town when I espied a hunt car follower who, taking pity, turned round and took me the rest of the way. I was back at the farmhouse rendezvous almost as quickly as those who had employed more orthodox means of transport.

One way and another it had been an entertaining day — what you might call a good tenpennyworth.

PAST MY PEAK?

There I was, on top of this rocky crag, for all the world like a chamois surveying his mountainous domain. Perhaps I have overdrawn the analogy a trifle, for in truth I was more like a damp chamois leather which, if you think about it, is only a chamois with all the stuffing knocked out of it. The reason for both my altitude and my exhaustion was my introduction to fell hunting, a pastime which combines sport and high speed mountaineering.

My guide for the occasion, a native of the area, treated the near vertical hillside with all the disdain of a London clubman breasting the slope of St James's Street on the way to his pre-luncheon dry martini. Not so his disciple. I lived at the time in a part of the country where a morning's work by any reasonably fit mole would qualify for a contour line on the map. To be transported suddenly into Himalayan-like terrain and be expected to scale the heights came as a bit of a shock to the nervous system. Still, if that New Zealand chap could reach the top of Everest without even the hope of finding a fox at the top, I was not going to be defeated.

Though I write when the sharper details of the nightmare climb are shrouded in the kindly mists of time, I can say in retrospect that the sense of achievement and the view of arrival at the top made it seem worthwhile. I can well understand the wild surmise with which stout Cortez surveyed the distant Pacific as he stood silent upon a peak in Darien. I doubt, however, if he suffered as much as stout Curtis

9

reaching his peak in Cumberland. Had he done so he would not have stood silent but, like me, he would have been lying there blowing like a grampus. At first, the glorious confusion of the fells tumbling away into the distance seemed more like ocean rollers about to pound a shipwrecked mariner on the rocks but gradually I got my breath back and was able to appreciate my surroundings.

Not for long, though. A large sandy-coloured dog fox, the killer (so I was told later) of many a lamb, slipped through the rocks beneath us and set his mask for the valley below. He was shortly followed by hounds, the huntsman, the field and, perforce, by me. Immediately I found myself in even more trouble. My legs, reduced to a sort of rubbery substance by the climb, were scarcely capable of supporting my body, let alone maintaining it in a vertical position during the descent. My return to the valley was therefore even less dignified than the climb out but a great deal quicker. At one point in my precipitate descent I disturbed a crow. I have no doubt that the startled caw it emitted as it leapt out of the way meant "Look out, chaps! There's fourteen stone of potential carrion on the way down." I did survive, but only just. The rest of the day I spent at valley level, content to watch the pursuit through my glasses.

As soon as I had accepted an invitation for a second visit to the fell country, I set about thinking of ways in which to survive the rigours of what promised to be a very energetic week. Short of enlisting the services of a couple of Sherpas, it seemed obvious that the frontal attack method I had employed previously was doomed to failure. I resorted instead to a stratagem which, with hindsight, I can recommend to others who may be short of wind and flabby of leg.

It involved picking the brains of some local hunter as to the likely lie of a fox and the direction of the first draw. One must then avoid the Meet and head straight for a suitable height which commands a view of the area. It is then possible to take one's time about achieving the chosen summit with plenty of pauses to admire the view and regain one's breath. The only equipment I have found essential to this form of hunting is a stick of good strong wood and a flask of good strong whisky.

Granted a fox in approximately the right place, one of two things may happen. Either he runs straight up the side on which one is standing, or he goes the other way. In the first case one has the pleasure of watching the other hunters, those made of sterner stuff or, perhaps, less gifted with foresight, toiling up towards one. In the latter case a glorious view can be had of the hunt as it develops along the opposite ridge. Eventually the hunt disappears and again one is faced with two alternatives, to descend and attempt to make contact again or to descend to the nearest pub.

The undoubted scenic pleasures of the fells are, to my mind, enhanced by the nomenclature employed throughout the district. Names such as Troutbeck recall hunting days long gone. Then, appropriately situated just north of Wordsworth's Cottage, are such poetic names as Stybarrow Dodd, Striding Edge and Dollywaggon Pike. On one drive I stopped to look up the name of a hill I was passing to discover that it had the charming name of Darling Fell. Round the next corner was a sign saying Darling How. Their juxtaposition seemed like a snippet of conversation overheard at a debutantes' ball, perhaps a discussion about some young lady's descent from grace.

If stamina is a requirement for the follower of fell fox hounds, no less is it an essential when hunting is over for the day. For the southerner, reference to a Hunt Ball or Hunt Dinner may conjure up visions of starched shirts, elegant tail coats, haute cuisine dishes, high fashion dresses and high-spirited cavortings on the ballroom floor.

In the fells, such is the frequency with which such celebrations are held, elegance and spaciousness have been discarded in favour of more practical clothing for the three main events of the evening — eating, drinking and singing. Had my constitution been capable of withstanding such an onslaught, I could have accepted invitations to a party every night of my stay — and one or two lunchtime ones as well.

Until I visited this part of the world I had always thought various writers' descriptions of tables and sideboards "groaning under the weight of food" as over-indulgence in the use of descriptive licence. No longer, not after attending a fell hunt dinner. Quite frankly, I would not have been surprised had the table at which I sat let out a scream of agony, such was the volume of edibles placed upon it. Veritable mountains of cream cakes, bread and butter, salads, jellies, gateaux and pastries rose high enough to prevent one seeing the person sitting opposite. Tier upon tier they rose like some pastrycook's vision of the fells themselves.

It was an astonishing sight, but no more so than the one which followed. Dinner was advertised as 7.30 for 8 pm. At 7.20 sharp the hungry hordes poured in and set about the tables like a demolition team working on double time. Well before the appointed hour for dinner the tables were bereft of all but a few crumbs. Only contented smiles and a few discreet burps were left as evidence of the achievement of this monster disappearing trick.

And then it was time for "a bit of a sing". The requirements are simple. Any room capable of holding about 50 people with a bar at one end will do. Then put about two hundred into it and start singing. There is no accompaniment and voice training is not a prerequisite. Most of the songs are in the form of long tales about huntsmen and hunting, interrupted only by rousing choruses and occasional noises from the direction of the bar. The latter are invariably followed by loud "Shushes" and calls for order from the Master of Ceremonies. And so the evening goes on. The atmosphere thickens, a distinct smell of damp terrier pervades the room, much beer is drunk and not a little spilt and the singing continues until well into the morning.

Long before the end, exhausted from a day's hunting, eating and drinking, I had crept away to my bed upstairs. Even the final chorus of Peel's View Halloo (rendered as only it can be in the. heart of John Peel's country), whatever it may have done to those in the cemetery or to foxes in their lairs, failed to disturb my subsequent slumbers.

INTRODUCING THE BEAKIES

Few people will have been lucky enough to read The Sporticus Book of Unusual Birds (published by Bobolink and Dowitcher). The original feather-bound, limited edition was not a success. A large number of copies were shot within a day or so of release and the pages were never retrieved; at least one was eaten by a dog and the remainder went into moult. A lesser black-backed edition was then produced but, in spite of being fully protected, sadly this too has become extinct.

Fortunately, I still have a copy of the book in my possession and thought it might be of interest to readers if I reproduced here some of the species depicted therein.

The Beakies appear here, in the appropriate Sections of this book, under the headings of Predatory Beakies, Game Beakies, Water Beakies and Migratory Beakies.

C.C.

RED-BREASTED HORNBLOWER   *(tallio tallio)*
The Hornblower is easily recognised by its bright scarlet body and black, rounded top of head. There are, however, some interesting variants reported in different parts of the country, notable the yellow-, blue- and grey-breasted, while there are also two types of green-breasted – one much slower moving.
Voice: A merry trumpeting. The most easily recognised calls are the urgent tootles it emits when in pursuit of its quarry and a longer, three note call (with the last note sustained) made just before it retires to roost. When aroused, the Hornblower is justly renowned for the wide variety of calls it can make and which usually cause all other birds nearby to fall silent. An example of one of these is *oldaarduruddifools.*
Habitat: Very wide-ranging in most parts of Britain with the exception of northern Scotland. It is usually followed by sometimes huge flocks of Thrusters, and Brown-Breasted Bowlers. Further behind, the keen observer will also note numbers of Hedge Larks, Hedge Cuckoos (or Stopcocks) and Flat-Capped Petrols. Note: There have, from time to time, been fears that this species might become extinct. However, it is still on the protected list and, happily, there appear to be more of these colourful birds to be seen in our countryside than ever before.

14

C.C.

GLOSSY-CRESTED THRUSTER   *(Celer maximus)*
This superb looking bird can be identified by its tall black glossy crest
and tremendous speed of flight, going long distances in a straight line.
The bird illustrated above is the Old English or Edwardian Thruster
which is now rare and can be distinguished from other varieties by the
swallow-tail. Both males and females have spurs, but only males have
the tall crest.
Voice: A loud chattering when gathered in flocks, but mostly silent
when in flight apart from the occasional *gerroutomiway.*
Habitat: Same as for the Hornblower with which it frequently
associates. The Thruster sometimes flies so fast that it outstrips the
Hornblower — never more than once in a day though.
When first seen in early autumn, the Thruster is in moult, drab in
colour and virtually flightless, almost indistinguishable from the
Ratcatcher or Brown-Breasted Bowler. It regains its full glorious
plumage and flight feathers early in November.

C.C.

SECRETARY BIRD *(capu capu)*
A sharp pair of eyes are needed to spot the Secretary Bird (or Capper, as it is sometimes known). With its round, black-topped head, and a red or black body, it hides among similarly plumaged birds while stalking its prey. Even the wariest of birds have been known to be fooled by its ability to go into sudden moult and then pounce from behind a hedge. Thus it often catches the nimble Stint.
Voice: Although a quiet bird, its voice has become noticeably more strident in recent years. Whereas, a short time ago it used to call *tenbobplees*, more urgent cries of *itsatenna* and even a repeated *twenti* and *twentifyv* have recently been recorded. Sometimes known to make a chinking sound while in flight.
Habitat: Its most frequently noted perch is near open gateways. A solitary bird, but usually moves around among Thrusters, Ratcatchers, etc. Resident birds normally escape its attentions, but migratory birds, particularly the late arrivals, often fall prey to the Capper.

16

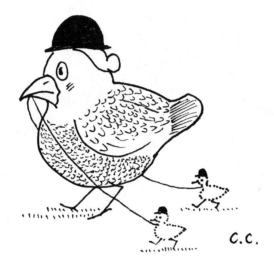

LEADING WREN   *(mater conducta)*
Although appearing in a variety of plumage, the Leading Wren can easily be identified since it is the only bird that keeps its young close to it at all times.
It is inclined to be broody. Males only seldom seen.
Voice: An almost continuous *cluck-cluck-cluck*, sometimes interspersed with a much sharper *keepyorneesin*.
Habitat: Although the Leading Wren is·occasionally sighted at other times of the year, the three or four weeks around Christmas are when they are most commonly seen. Take care though, the approach of larger birds causes the Leading Wren to become agitated and even, on occasions, quite aggressive when defending her still flightless young.

HEDGE CUCKOO   *(croppa frequentia)*
The Hedge Cuckoo (also known as the Stopcock) appears in many different plumages. Even the keenest birdwatcher may fail to spot this species as it is usually far away from other birds of the field. But, once seen, it can be quickly identified by its erratic cross-country flight and its repeated swoops at hedges, ditches and walls. When it finally flies over a hedge, more often than not it dives down to the ground. It can also be seen zig-zagging across country through gateways and gaps left in hedges by the passage of other birds.
Voice: The alarm cry, made as it dives towards the ground, can best be described as a loud wail. On the approach to a hedge there can often be heard a small plaintive cry. Once on the ground it tends to run round in small circles chirping *havuseenmihaws?*
Habitat: Widespread. Often feeds in hedges and frequently observed in the bottoms of ditches. Usually retires to roost early in the day.

18

C.C.

SHAGGY-CRESTED TWIT   *(versus vulpicidi)*
Apart from the bearded variety (shown above), males and females are
virtually indistinguishable, both having long untidy crests. Very
aggressive towards some other species, notably the Hornblower.
Voice: Emits loud raucous cries while flapping its wings wildly. Has
been known to imitate the Holler and the Hornblower. In urban
surroundings it has also been heard to make repeated cries of
banthebom and *eenochout*.
Habitat: A resident of towns and cities, small groups of Twits make
occasional forays into the countryside, mainly in the southern counties
of England. These flocks of almost entirely young birds can be very
aggressive but usually disperse when other birds disregard them.

The 20th

They call me Charles James and a few other names,
Such as Reynard and Charlie the Fox.
I'm a glutton for hens and for turkeys in pens
And a worry to men who tend flocks.

People cut quite a dash and they pay out good cash
When it's me that they're huntin' y'know.
I'm a hell of a fellow, just hear how they bellow,
"Forrard on!" — "Gone away!" — "Tally ho!"

Century Fox

Hounds and horses all rush in pursuit of my brush
When, with hats raised, they shout, "Gone away!"
Then I lead hounds a dance and they haven't a chance,
For I know they'll not catch me today.

When the day's sport is done and they've all had their fun,
Do you know what I'm going to do?
First, I'll dine on a pheasant and my dreams will be pleasant,
For hunting is **my** pleasure, too.

21

They're Back!

As I lean on the gate, I say, "Ponies just wait!
Make the most of that grass while you can.
From now on each day it's a netful of hay
And a handful of nuts and some bran.

"Yes, those darlings are back and they're cleaning their tack,
So just you take heed of my warning.
They're back for the holidays, Christmas and jolly days
And we're off to the meet in the morning!"

"Mummy! Somebody's sat on the brim of my hat."
"Where my hairnet?" the other one yells.
And then there's a panic when something organic
Is found it a boot—and it smells.

With a popping of stitches they squeeze in their breeches
And boots which are sizes too small,
Then a pony gets free. It's a wonder to me
That they ever get hunting at all.

At the meet there's a dash and gone in a flash
Are the trayfuls of food and the port.
And there's one little lad (he takes after dad)
Who drinks a lot more than he ought.

Says the General to me, "Got the brats out I see.
There'll be trouble today to be sure."
At once he's proved right when, his horse, taking fright,
Bucks him off in a heap of manure.

At the very first fence, rushing hither and thence,
The ponies go faster and faster.
With pigtails a-flying two girls fall off crying
While a third gallops under the Master.

With his face turning black, the Master rides back.
Shouts a squeaky voice, "Make way for Sir!"
But a Shetland defeats him and promptly unseats him,
Its leading rein caught round his spur.

By a quarter to two there are only a few
Still attempting to follow the horn.
The rest have got cold, fallen off or been told
To go home in a rage—and they've gorn.

Her tummy is aching, So Mummy is taking
The younger one back in the box.
But somewhere or other, I fear that her brother
Is still in pursuit of the fox.

I seek him in vain over hill, farm and lane
Till it's dark and my temper is thin.
But then with a rush he comes up with the brush
And from one ear to t'other a grin.

With the hols just begun and with miles yet to run
In pursuit on my feet like a fool,
It isn't the **sheep** that I count going to sleep
But the **days** till they go back to school.

23

Costume Piece

If a hunter true you'd be,
Listen carefully to me...

Never, never let your dress
Be incorrect or, worse, a mess.
You can be both smart and warm
In proper hunting uniform.

A hunting cap should not be worn
Unless you are to farming born.
Upon your head if you fall flat
Should be a top or bowler hat.

In spite of risk of hat detached,
To coat it should not be attached.
Your stock should always be of white,
Its plain pin set from left to right.

A coat of black and boots of brown
To Master's face will bring a frown.
Nor, lest you might be thought a scrubber,
Should your boots be made of rubber.

All boots need a pair of spurs—
A larger pair for his than hers—
And then, above, a little gap
'Twixt top of boot and garter strap.

A slapping whip is surely wrong,
You need one with a lash and thong.
And gloves you really ought to wear
(Take, just in case, a second pair).

Though purists say not strictly normal,
You are allowed to wear less formal
Tweed coats, brown boots and bowler hats—
As worn by men for catching rats.

So, when you ride up to the Meet,
Let all those standing on their feet
Say, as of you they first catch sight:
"By gum! That chap—he's turned out right!"

With apologies to the late Mark Beaufoy, whose immortal lines "A Father's Advice" should be engraved in the minds of all who use a shotgun.

See Ho!

A merry sight the beaglers are,
With hounds and huntsman ranging far.
The woods and hills throw back the sounds
Of horn and music of the hounds
            when beagling.

To follow hounds and hunt the hare
Of feet you only need a pair.
Their age no matter, man and boy
Can walk or run and both enjoy
            their beagling.

Dukes and dustmen, men of riches,
Men who mend the council ditches,
Without a horse or rod or gun,
They one and all enjoy the fun
            of beagling.

When, after several years of this,
Rheumatic pains reduce the bliss,
Don't give it up, for here's a thought
How you can still enjoy the sport
            of beagling.

When panting far behind, alone,
Take heart! For reasons quite unknown,
The hare, her mind on other things,
When chased will often run in rings
            round beagling.

So if, through age or lacking puff,
You feel that you have had enough
But still desire to view the chase,
You may, from some superior place,
     watch beagling.

As round and round the hunters go,
Just sit and watch them down below.
Imbibing whisky from a flask,
One wonders—what more could one ask
     of beagling?

Then, if by chance the chase moves on
And from one's view the hunt has gone,
The nearest inn's not far to walk
And later there they'll sing and talk
     of beagling.

So, whether you prefer to run,
Or walk, or sit, you'll find it's fun.
A hare's afoot, they cry: "See Ho!"
There is no finer sport, I know,
     than beagling.

EGYPTIAN DUCK

The first Jumbo I ever saw on a runway was not packed with more than 300 tourists; it was large, grey, pachydermatous, accompanied by about twenty of its fellows and had to be shepherded away by Air Traffic Control before I could effect a landing. I believe that the runway concerned no longer consists of the local soil, nor is it lined, as it often was, by very tall, stark naked natives of the most extraordinary physical proportions, on the exact details of which there is no need to dwell here. It, the runway that is, now extends for about two miles, is made of concrete and the elephants have long since departed.

From the foregoing you will have gathered that the period of which I write is not in the immediate past. No, it was not that long ago; it was, in fact, barely thirty years since. Such is the rate of progress.

I was, at the time, based in Egypt with a ground attack fighter squadron and our sphere of influence included the Sudan, wherein dwelt the elephants. On our return to Egypt, I was delighted to find that I, though a mere Pilot Officer (the lowest of the low, in case you are not familiar with Royal Air Force ranks), had qualified for a day's duck shooting with the Embassy Shoot. This piece of information may not cause you any surprise, but I can assure you that the lowest Army rank normally to qualify for this splendid affair was full Colonel – and there were not too many of them either. My good fortune lay in the fact that there happened to be a dearth of sporting RAF officers in the Canal Zone at the time.

The venue for the shoot was a marshy area, to the left and up a bit on the map from Tel el Kebir, itself a fairly godforsaken spot. Weekly, during the season, two parties set out towards what for duckshooters, but no one else, was a truly delectable spot. One party, headed by the ambassadorial Rolls, came from the west, the other, trailing in the dust left by the G.O.C.'s Humber, came from Ismailia.

As befitted my lowly position, I found myself in the rearmost Jeep of the westbound convoy, struggling to maintain contact, first in the dark and later through clouds of billowing sand. When we finally arrived, there was no drawing for places, which were allocated strictly according to rank. I therefore had an extremely long walk to my hide which turned out to be, by any standards, a very luxurious edifice, with a floor of firm boards raised above the water and surrounded by well bound reeds. The snag to this splendid appointment was having to share it with a filthy, evil-smelling wallah who had been deputed as my head bearer for the day; yes, there was an underling, but his task was to retrieve, spending his time between successful shots standing up to his waist in water some distance away.

The signal for the start of the shoot was the firing of a cannon mounted on a boat in the lake which formed the centre of the marsh. Nowadays the same sound would doubtless send several flights of supersonic fighter aircraft airward, but in this case it caused several thousand ducks to become airborne. Immediately a furious fusillade broke out from the butts in the favoured central positions. It was some time before my first chance came and, in the meantime, I had to suffer the unwelcome attentions of my appointed assistant. In addition to the already mentioned smell, a continual coughing, interspersed with the occasional ill-directed spit, came from him. A further distraction was his incessant demands for "ceegareets" and his obvious designs on my cartridge bag did nothing to help my concentration.

I therefore missed my first few chances at duck, but eventually started taking a few shots. As soon as the first success was registered, assistant no 2, galabeer awash, came splashing out to retrieve, thereby effectively scaring away every duck within sight, of which by then there was a considerable number.

For the next three hours, flights of duck, expletions of betel juice from between two blackened teeth onto my feet and the weird cavortings of my retriever, alternated in roughly equal proportions. Sharp at midday shooting ceased and the time had come for me to dispense 'bakhshish' — a tip — to my two companions, I can hardly call them helpers. Custom dictated that I donated the lot to No 1, with whom I had unwillingly shared my butt for three hours and who had done nothing to increase my enjoyment of the day. I am absolutely certain that No 2 saw nothing of it — and he at least had tried.

The long walk back — No 2 encumbered with the bag, myself with gun and cartridge bag, neither of which I trusted with No 1 — terminated with our arrival at a numbered peg, alongside which the results of one's efforts had to be deposited for all to see. Such had been the barrage from the hides nearest the centre, that I fully expected my own modest tally to cause some merriment. Cartridges were, in those days, extremely cheap. Even so, I was amazed (and not asked again) to find that I had shot more than some of those in the favoured places — and I am not a very good shot.

There was another, less illustrious, shoot, not far removed from the Embassy Shoot. This was known as the B.T.E. (British Troops in Egypt) Shoot. Again to my surprise I found myself offered a place. Shooting times being different, it was considered necessary for this occasion to spend the night prior to shooting in a tented encampment adjacent to the following morning's sport. Suitably equipped, as I thought, for a day's sport, I proceeded thither. I was only slightly alarmed to find myself being conducted to an immaculate tent by an equally immaculate batman and to be informed that dinner was to be served at 8pm in the mess tent. That my alarm increased considerably on my entry to said tent at the appointed hour will be understood when I tell you that I was ushered in by a gloved and white-jacketed steward towards a dinner-jacketed Brigadier (I was by then a Flying Officer) and the smartest part of my apparel was an off-white rollneck sweater.

Worse was to follow. The seating arrangements somehow contrived to place me opposite to the Brigadier's personal guest, a large floribund man, my instant dislike of whom I managed to conceal during the meal by maintaining a discreet silence. Throughout dinner, the conversation centred around the relative merits of various types of cartridges and, in order to remain as unobtrusive as possible, I avoided joining in by imbibing quantities of wine which circulated at frequent intervals. The port was my undoing. It was while I was quietly sipping my third — or was it my fourth? — glass, that the Brigadier's guest, who had just proclaimed loudly that his cartridges were specially shipped to him by a very well known London gunmaker, leant towards me and asked what cartridges I favoured.

One less glass of port and a modicum of discretion would have produced a different answer. As it was I told the truth.

"Trap-shooting cartridges", I replied, for they were virtually free at the time.

There was what can best be described as a sort of 'Harrumph' from the other side of the table, conversation changed to other matters and, shortly afterwards, I chose a suitable moment to retire.

The procedure the following day was roughly the same as on the Embassy Shoot, only on a less extravagant scale. To my intense relief I found that I was not allocated any native assistants so I proceeded to my far flung post unaccompanied. This in turn resulted in my having to return to the central point carrying my own, consequently larger, share of the spoils. Modesty, not to mention a poor memory, prevents me from telling you what my bag was. My recollection is entirely clear however, that opposite the numbered peg of the gentleman sitting across the table from me the night before, was lying a single, rather bedraggled teal.

Perhaps it was as well that the distance I had to travel to register my tally was sufficient to allow the departure of the more senior members before I arrived on the scene. Otherwise I might have said something else I regretted.

A GLORIOUS FAILURE

The success of gossip writers depends largely on their having larders well stocked with juicy titbits, from which they can select suitable morsels for the daily delectation of their readers. Thus, over coffee and cornflakes, one is able also to satisfy one's appetite for the affairs and affaires of the rich and titled.

While most of such writings are produced on a day-to-day basis, they are punctuated with great relish by a number of annual events, for which special sections of the columnists' larders are reserved. No section is better stocked with well chewed cliches than that marked August 12. Every year the same old truisms – and the same old falsisms, for that matter – are dutifully trotted out. The date is never anything but glorious and the moors continue to reverberate to the crash of rifle fire, etc, etc.

Thus it is that the impression is widely held of grouse moors teeming with senior officials of the Conservative Party and the higher echelons of the aristocracy, with as many multi-millionaires as possible squeezed into any butts not already occupied by members of the first two categories. With the assistance of a pair of best British guns each, these gentlemen will soon be speeding thousands of grouse carcasses to the premier restaurants of the world.

Nor does responsibility for the presentation of this quaint and totally inaccurate picture, I regret, lie solely with the gossip writers. Not long ago I read a piece by a columnist on animal affairs (who should know better) in a daily paper (which should also know better) which referred to August 12 as "the day when it becomes legitimate for millionaires to slaughter grouse". How evocative is that word "slaughter" and how beloved it is of quasi-conservationists and others hell-bent on the destruction of field sports.

But, enough of philosophising! The moor on which I have been lucky enough to spend the opening days of the last few grouse seasons is not one of those frequented by Rolls-Roycefuls of shipping magnates. I have yet to hear an election address being practised in the next butt and the chance of seeing the glitter of sunlight reflected in a ducal coronet is, I would have thought, remote in the extreme. There is, mind you, good reason for this lack of noble patronage.

I can well remember (indeed, who could forget?) the first drive of the very first season. When we had reached the moor, after a hair-raising ride up a track that was only barely navigable, our eyes feasted themselves on a veritable wealth of healthy heather and we leapt from the Land-Rovers in high spirits. The talk at lower levels had all been about many years of neglect leading to poor prospects, but this was forgotten in a purple haze of optimism. With that much heather, there had to be grouse about.

The draw for places was made and we settled into our respective butts with eager expectancy. While it is true to say that all branches of field sports involve a period of waiting and require a high degree of patience in the participants — whether they be fishermen, hunters or wildfowlers — there is none that I know to compare with the nerve tingling suspense of waiting for the first covey of grouse to appear. This was a particularly long drive and time marched on leaden feet.

Suddenly and with an unexpectedness that brought instant alertness, there came a shout. There are other months of the year and other places far removed from a grouse moor when and where I would have been delighted to hear that yell. It was, in fact, a holloa and over the moor with a graceful lolloping stride came a beautiful golden-coloured fox. It was followed at intervals by other members of the same family. Not a bird came forward, unless you count the crows which, with contented smiles on their faces after a surfeit of grouse chicks and eggs, passed in a steady stream like over-fed diners leaving a restaurant at closing time. The drive concluded with a rather bemused flock of black-faced sheep being shepherded past the butts by the beaters.

The second, return drive was virtually a carbon copy of the first. Charles James and family were once again the first to appear, hastened on their way this time by an exasperated gentleman in number eight butt, who seized the chance to discharge his weapon for the first time that day. Only the crows were absent, possibly digesting their illgotten gains over the corvine equivalent of a decanter of port in a place undisturbed by the intrusions of man. Panting a bit by this time, the sheep made the return journey through the butts. I swear one old ram shook his head sadly at me as he passed by.

Succeeding drives were little more successful than the first two and the day's bag, towards which, incidentally, I did not contribute, was minimal.

The following day, which had been set aside for walking up, promised to be a real scorcher. The sun shone out of a cloudless sky, birds twittered in the trees and, by the time we had finished breakfast, a shimmering heat haze was rising from the hills opposite. I felt dreadful. The previous evening, what with a unanimous desire to wash away the day's woes and a lengthy discussion of the morrow's plans, the profits of a number of distilleries had been considerably enhanced. By closing time the prospect of a day's walk after grouse had held no more terrors than that of a post-prandial stroll round St. James's Park.

Now it was different. The moment of starting on a 20-mile slog through a bog-ridden, heather-filled sauna, carrying a gun, game-bag and hangover was upon us. The reality was, if possible, worse than the expectation.

Many years ago an ungrateful Air Ministry saw fit to despatch me to a part of the world where a gentleman with the unlikely title of the Imam of Oman was, for some reason best known to himself, disputing the ownership of a particularly unattractive piece of desert with the Sultan of Muscat and Oman. On one occasion during the campaign in which I found myself involved, I also found myself alone in the desert in a Land-Rover with a leaking radiator, on a day when the shade temperature passed the 130 degrees Fahrenheit mark. My distress then was never matched again until that day on top of a grouse moor.

The only member of the party who was not noticeably suffering from the heat was Sweep, a flat-coated retriever belonging to my host. Under other circumstances Sweep's turn of speed and incredible stamina might have been attributes to admire. As it was, he ensured that the few grouse not lying prostrate from heat became airborne anything up to half a mile ahead. Occasionally another, alarmed by the infuriated shouts emanating from Sweep's owner, also took flight well out of shot. Remarkably, we did each manage to get a bird or two — and I mean that literally. Some got one and others got two.

And so two memorable days came to a hot and sticky ending. I would like to be able to report that things were much better the following year. Sadly, I am unable to do so. True, the ranks of predators had noticeably thinned, but the extra grouse resulting from this reduction were blown away by gales of wind on the driving day and escaped virtually unscathed.

As the wind swept the moor on the first day, so Sweep swept it on the second. A year older maybe, but not one bit less energetic and, if anything, a shade more deaf to his master's loud and frequent requests for his immediate return. Still, we did manage to collect a few brace before returning, tired but reasonably happy, to base camp.

Succeeding years have not brought any noticeable increase in the bags but those two first days of the grouse season are still the most eagerly anticipated in my calendar. I only wish some of those gossip-writers could be there.

OVER THE HILL

Like all sports, stalking has its own terminology which it behoves the beginner to learn if he is to avoid mistakes which might spoil his enjoyment. In the case of Highland stalking, the strange new words are the harder to comprehend, often being spoken out of the corner of the mouth in a thick Scottish accent and usually into the teeth of a gale.

Here, then, is a short glossary of some of the terms, the interpretation of which I learned through hard experience:-

Hill A precipitous mountain, the top of which is invariably hidden by cloud

Wee bit of a breeze A gale

Mist (pronounced must) When you can see absolutely nothing

Missed (pronounced must) Your eyes need testing

Path A Scottish joke word for the route you take up the hill

Piece A packed lunch carried in the pocket which, after a stalk, is inextricably mixed with the other contents and usually contains at least one bullet

Gralloch What is removed from a dead stag just as you were about to start on your piece

Drag Pulling a stag's carcase over almost impassable ground (N.B. It has nothing to do with Danny la Rue in a tartan frock)

Monarch A stag (cf Landseer's glen)

Muttony monarch A stag which, on closer inspection, turns out to be a sheep

Damned grouse An unsporting bird that jumps up and spoils a stalk

Face (1) The side of a hill

Face (2) That which, when exposed to Face (1), clears it of deer

The Rifle Not, as you might imagine, a weapon, but the person who pulls the trigger. The title 'Stalker' is reserved for the chap who knows what he is doing.

Forest A very large tract of land entirely devoid of trees

Donald Due to a shortage of christian names in Scotland, most of the stalkers, pony boys, ponies and probably many of the stags all have the same name. In my case it was Donald, you may find a preponderance of Willies, Ewans or Iains

Foot Five toes and a heel held together by blisters

For my first attempt at stalking, preceded by the inevitable Donald, I was led up the sort of slope I consider suitable only for mountain goats, extremely fit Sherpas or, possibly, for me in a funicular. It was not long before my legs, unaccustomed to near vertical progression, started to complain and my lungs, no doubt astonished by sudden inrushes of Highland air, wheezed painfully. Frequent dizzy spells beset me. Only the sight of Donald's remorselessly lifting boots kept me going.

During the climb one's hopes are continually raised by apparently being able to see the summit not far ahead. Having reached this goal, it can then be seen that there is another 'summit' ahead, then another and another. Like the oasis in a mirage, it retreats before one. At last we did reach the top after an ascent that Donald described as 'quite a nice wee climb'. There was still quite a way to go but, with the going considerably easier, it was possible to enjoy the surroundings.

From the heather, grouse, singly and in coveys, continually jumped – their 'go-back, go-back, back, back' seeming to voice their resentment at our intrusion. Ptarmigan, still in summer plumage, golden plover and the odd snipe could also be seen. Once, a sudden familiar sound had me scanning the sky keenly until I spotted a skein of greylag geese tumbling out of the clouds and arguing loudly about which direction they should take. Their sudden appearance startled a distant party of deer into panicky flight. A little later we had a superb view of a golden eagle as it swept past on fixed wings, causing Donald to remark: "I wouldna mind becoming one of those in my next life." Somewhere beneath that leathery exterior beat a romantic's heart.

Wildfowlers and fishermen in particular will know what I mean when I say that the time spent actually in close pursuit of one's quarry is minimal compared with that spent in preparation and in just waiting. Indeed, this applies to most field sports, none more than stalking. The long climb and the subsequent search for a suitable beast can take several hours, the actual stalk may be of only a few minutes duration, or, as in the case of my first stag, no time at all.

A number of watchful hinds were between the possible target Donald had spotted and ourselves and it was while trying to circumnavigate these sentinels that I suddenly found myself eyeball to eyeball with one. I had not earlier appreciated that the route Donald had chosen, while perfectly adequate to conceal his diminutive self, left a portion of my much larger frame exposed.

"Whissht!" I whispered as I sank to the ground. At least 'whissht' (a useful Scottish alarm signal I had picked up) was what I meant to say, but my false teeth slipped and it came out as more of a 'phlutt'. Anyway it had the desired effect.

"What is it?" asked Donald, probably thinking I needed yet another stop to rest my limbs.

"There's a large hind just ahead," I replied in a whisper, having readjusted my dentures.

"Damn," muttered Donald, "We'd better hide bide a wee, before trying to move round her."

Having bided whatever constitutes a wee, Donald inched himself up the bank, spent a moment or two peering over the top and then returned in a state of great excitement.

"That's nae heend, mon, it's a ruddy great hummel."

My heart sank. A 'hummel', to a chap with visions of a many-pointed hatrack in the hall, is about as popular as a bald man in a hairdressers – and equally rare. It is, in fact a hornless stag, which must speedily be disposed of before it produces progeny of the same ilk. All I had to do was move a yard or two with reasonable care and Donald was ecstatic at the result of my first shot at a stag. There were to be no more chances that day and, somewhat despondently, legs aching and barely able to support me, I was back in the Lodge.

However, the restorative effects of a glass or two of Scotland's favourite tipple are remarkable. In no time at all, I was boring everyone to death with highly exaggerated accounts of my achievement. They must have been mightily relieved when I finally retired to bed flushed, I have to admit, not only with success.

On waking the next morning I appreciated for the first time what the expression 'he's gone over the hill' really means. I was there. I felt very old indeed, every limb throbbed with pain and the act of getting out of bed required quite an effort. Dressing and pulling socks over badly blistered feet was agony and, as for donning my boots ... printable words fail me. All this had to be borne because that day there was another hill to climb and, perhaps, another stag to be shot.

Thankfully, the climb was less severe, although, due to the injuries I had sustained the day before, no less painful. Remarkably too, the Stalker allocated to me was not only not called Donald but was female. No matter, the result was exactly the same. I shot another hummel.

My account of the day's proceedings received noticeably greater respect that evening. I was, after all, on my way to becoming Scotland's greatest expert on hornless stag shooting. We had been joined by the ducal Laird who, after expressing initial incredulity, consulted the record books. These confirmed that hummels had only rarely been seen in the forest, still less shot, over many years.

Only the presence of a witness, yet another Donald, allows me to relate that, on alighting from the Land Rover at the head of the glen on the third morning, I put up my fieldglasses and sharply into focus came — a hummel. The only reason my name does not appear in the Guinness Book of Records is because that one managed to outmanoeuvre us.

I would like to take my hat off to those whose expertise at stalking has been rewarded by visible and tangible results. The trouble is, I still have nowhere to hang it.

TWEEDIE DAPPER   *(frequentia syndicatus)*
The British native Dapper (seen here on its usual perch) is rather drab in appearance, though foreign visitors of the same species tend to be much more gaudy in their plumage. The Tweedie Dapper can easily be recognised by its habit of gathering in small flocks of eight or ten, then separating and sitting motionless for long periods about 30 yards apart.
Voice: A rather drawn out *ovah* (not to be confused with the Common Ruff's more abrupt *ova*). In January the Dapper's call tends to change slightly to *cokovah.*
Habitat: First sightings usually occur on or around August 12 on moorlands in Scotland and the north of England. In September the Dapper migrates to lower ground, mostly open farmland, before moving into woodlands during the winter months. Last sightings are towards the end of January, after which the Dapper disappears from the country scene.

C.C.

POT-BELLIED PUFFIN *(weesi rotunda)*
The Pot-Bellied Puffin is a large ungainly bird which, during the short periods it can be seen in the country, often appears in the richly checkered plumage shown here.
Voice: Generally a sort of wheezing sound when in motion. When it stops it often calls *hangonaminit* or *isaysteddionthairoldboi.*
Habitat: Being a bird normally resident in towns and cities, the Puffin has difficulty in adapting itself to conditions in the countryside where it goes in search of a change of diet. Its usual food in towns is bread, of which it consumes far more than its fair share. Why it should change its normal habitat for the steep-sided moors and hills of the north is not known.

MUD OOZEL   *(quackus quackicidi)*

The Mud Oozel is a foreshore wader. It is not easy to see, being well camouflaged by its plumage which blends in well with its surroundings. Can sometimes be spotted on its way to and from its feeding place at dawn and dusk. Often spends hours away from the nest, comes back without having caught any food, spreads mud in and around the nest and gets hell from its mate.

Voice: Male, apart from an occasional *wagbi-wagbi,* is usually silent. The female utters loud and strident cries when greeting her mate, such as *dontputmuddonminicekleenflaw* and *taykurbootsoffatwunz.*

Habitat: From early September until mid-February the Mud Oozel can be seen in search of food between the high and low water marks on the foreshore almost anywhere round the coasts of Britain. It is not known where these birds go during the remaining months of the year.

A VERY OLD PHEASANT

I'm a very old pheasant and the reason I'm present
When most of my friends have been eaten?
I always remember, from the first of November,
*To **walk** when the coverts are beaten.*

Hi Lost!

Oh, the dogs on our shoot! "Will you come here, you brute!"
You can hear them shout all down the line.
Untrained and unruly, I promise you truly
That the only exception is mine.

There's old Colonel Jack, swearing, flat on his back
With his gun pointing up in the air.
You can hear how he felt when, attached to his belt,
His young labrador spotted a hare.

Dick's bird hits the ground, four dogs make a bound
And arrive on the scene all together.
They divide it in three and, from what I can see,
Dick's dog brings him back just one feather.

That spaniel of Joe's has a terrible nose,
A fact which accounts for the reason
Why he mutters rude words as he looks for his birds
—His dog hasn't found one all season.

"Get away from my bitch!" That's Fred's springer which,
(Apart from being too over-sexed)
Getting quite overwrought, drops each bird that it's caught
Before dashing straight on to the next.

Bob's not been too clever and used as a tether
His cartridge bag fixed to a stake.
When a rabbit went past, his dog took off fast
With his bag—now they're both in the lake.

I cannot believe a worse golden retriever
Exists than the one owned by Jones.
The only sound heard when it picks up a bird
Is a horrible crunching of bones.

But even that's better than Charlie's red setter,
Which is really the worst of the bunch.
After eating a pheasant, it did something unpleasant
While we all sat around having lunch.

Quite deaf to Jane's yell, like a bat out of hell
Goes her flat-coated dog being active
In pursuit of a runner and, though Jane is a stunner,
Her dog I find far from attractive.

No, you cannot dispute that the dogs on our shoot
Are the worst ever seen in a line.
Look, there goes one now and it's chasing a cow,
Disgraceful! Good gracious, it's mine!

Covert Charge

With costs ever steeper, the life of a Keeper—
It is not what it was, I'm afraid.
Now, instead of some earls and their debutante girls,
We have eight paying guns, all in trade.

Number one gun this week, who's in shipping and Greek,
Fires a hundred and twenty-three times.
All he gets for his trouble is a curious double
Of a dog and a beater called Grimes.

The young man number two has got something to do
With the City and comes here by air.
Although I have heard he has shares in James Purdey,
In the bag he does not have a share.

There's a butcher at three and it's quite plain to see
That he's not been before to a shoot.
He has just blown to bits a hen thrush and two tits
And then carved up a stationary coot.

Next to him is a brewer who, at lunch, had no fewer
Than five gins, which he drank much too quick.
In the best place at four, he is starting to snore
When he hiccoughs and falls off his stick.

Not one bird takes a dive as they pour over five,
Not a shot does the fishmonger fire.
A crab in his diet has caused some disquiet
And has made him discreetly retire.

Just beyond those two ricks is a tailor, at six,
Who is neatly turned out in bespoke.
Having opened his score with a shot in the straw.
There's a baa! when he lets off his choke.

A distiller from Fife, drawn seven, has a wife
Who is Spanish and all through the drive,
When he raises his gun, shouts "You no shoot zat one!
He's so preety, I like heem alive."

With a pump gun at eight's an oil man from the States,
Wearing clothes such as I've never seen.
At each bird that goes past there's a long drawn out blast,
When he empties a full magazine.

I am sorry to say, at the end of the day
When I lay out the bag on the ground,
Even counting poor Grimes and a bird shot ten times,
There is not quite enough to go round.

Deer, Oh Dear!

I agree that a stag looks at home on a crag
In the forest of which he's a denizen.
But his antlers look grand in **my** home as a stand
For my hats—and I'm partial to venison.

Mind you, going stalking is not merely walking
Through heather, then lying down flat
And just firing a shot—I assure you it's not—
There is rather more to it than that.

If, like me, you're not fit, or habitually sit
In an office or watching T.V.
Then stalking's a sport I suggest that you ought
To forget ... Look what happened to me!

For a start there's the 'hill', which I climb up until
I'm on top of a very large mountain,
Where the 'mist' (fog to you) first erases the view
And then drenches us all like a fountain.

48

My task's but a trifle for I am the 'Rifle',
With nothing to do but the firing;
It's the Stalker, of course, and the man with the horse
Who work—I just follow, perspiring.

'We'll just have a wee spy," I sink down with a sigh,
For I'm aching and starting to wilt.
(A 'wee spy' is a peer through the 'glass' for a deer,
Not a mini James Bond in a kilt).

When we've sighted a beast, still to
go there's at least
Half a mile, mostly flat on my tum,
While the burn water leaks through
the top of my breeks,
Making parts of me frigidly numb.

I look over a 'hag' and line up on a stag,
But then—what a horrid surprise!
At le moment critique with the stock in my cheek,
From the heather two ramblers arise.

As the hill clears of deer, "They shuild no do that here,"
Says the Stalker, "We'll have to retire."
There'll be no stag today." So we three wend our way
To the Lodge and a dram by the fire.

"What a beautiful stand—don't those antlers look grand!"
(I've gone up in my neighbours' esteem).
"Yes, it makes a good show—it's a Royal, you know."
But, alas! it is all still a dream.

Out for a Duck

I am shaken alive when, at quarter to five,
The alarm starts my labrador howling;
This in turn wakes the baby and I wonder if, maybe,
It is **not** *the right day to go fowling.*

It's two hours to the dawn of a January morn
And, regretting the evening before,
I get dressed in a rush without razor or brush
In my haste to be down on the shore.

Though the weather is right for a good morning flight,
Why on earth am I not still in bed?
Outside it is blowing and freezing and snowing
And, darn it!—the battery's dead.

But, at last, I'm away and the sky's not yet grey
As I drive to the top of the tide.
Then I wade through the mud, creeks and gullies and flood
Until finally reaching my hide.

Very soon I'm in luck, for here come some duck
Fast and low and I'll have to be quick;
So I swing on a bird, but the only sound heard
Is an almost inaudible click.

I let out a curse and, to make matters worse,
My dog disappears at the run,
Chasing birds I'd have shot if I hadn't forgot
To put cartridges into my gun.

Since my flask is still full, I am taking a pull
(To put back some fire in my belly)
When I hear a quick quack, turn and take a pace back
Into water that fills up my welly.

It's a marvellous sight as it starts to get light,
Though I'm not, I confess, overjoyed;
Gulls and dunlin abound and the sky's full of sound,
But of duck it's entirely devoid.

Now the tide's on the turn and I'm forced to return
From a morning I'd rather forget.
As I squelch through the door—"Don't put mud on my floor!"
And—"How many duck did you get?"

Wildfowling is fun for man with his gun,
Just like cricket—a wonderful sport.
But, when you're out of luck and you're out for a duck,
All that goes in the book is a nought.

FISH, FLESH & FOUL

No-one, even by the wildest stretch of imagination, could classify me as an expert fisherman. The only knots that I can tie really efficiently are those that appear two or three inches from the end of my cast with a dismal and unfailing regularity. It was therefore with a fair degree of trepidation that I allowed myself to be persuaded into a night fishing expedition after sea-trout (or, as they are known in those parts, "sewin") in the River Towy in Carmarthenshire.

My host was one of the keenest fishermen alive and with the ability to transmit his enthusiasm to others. In no time at all he had rigged me out in a pair of waders, pressed a rod and net into my hands and we were off to the river down a pitch black, thickly wooded and very steep hill. Impeded as I was by waders which were too short for me, my progress was a lumbering, stumbling scramble punctuated by frequent stops every time my rod got caught in some unseen hazard. Eventually, however, we made it to the bank.

Lack of wind and the bright full moon made it possible to see and hear fish jumping all over the place and it was with pleasurable anticipation that I gingerly eased myself into the water, the aim being to get far enough out to be able to cast right across the river. Everywhere around me fish were leaping from the water, the smaller ones with their tails aquiver producing a noise not unlike a drumming snipe. One big one, disdainful of my presence (he had, I must admit, little to fear) heaved himself out of the swift-flowing current almost at my elbow.

His silvery body flashed in the moonlight and he seemed to hang suspended in mid-air for a moment before dropping back with a resounding splash that drenched my face.

My technique, if that is not too daring a word to use, failed to produce anything to put into my net, although I did get a couple of nibbles. My total score that night added up to one hat, one left ear lobe, two vicious swipes on the back of the neck and several leaves off the far bank. At least the latter showed I was reaching the far side. In a mean sort of way, I was quite pleased to find that my host had only managed to catch one himself. After all, he was the expert and it would have been rude to outfish my host.

The return journey to the house was even more fraught with danger than the outward one. The moonlight by now was pale and the shadows deep. If you have ever tried walking uphill in a pair of waders that are too small, you will appreciate why I was quite pleased not to be carrying a heavy basket of fish. A forward and upward movement of the knee tightens the backside of the waders round one's own. This has the effect of snapping the foot down on the ground again which, in turn, brings the body sharply forward. It feels rather as though one is being manipulated by a very inept puppeteer on strings that have been cut to unequal lengths. After what seemed an age, we eventually regained the house where I fell thankfully into bed.

During my short stay in Wales, I was lucky enough to fit in another visit to the river, this time in daylight. Able at last to see where I was going, I strode out into the river, anxious to do better this time and bearing in mind the old Scottish adage "You'll no be catching any fush wi'out your fly in the water." My guide and mentor was giving me advice from the bank but my impatience and the rushing water carried his words out of earshot. The words "You ought to ..." came faintly over the water before the river closed over my head as I stepped into a pool and sank without trace. I surfaced in time to hear "... shallower a bit further down." Undeterred by a large section of the Towy swilling about in my waders, I started hopefully to drop my fly where I had been told and within a few minutes I had my first ever sea-trout in the net. Over-confidence caused me to lose several others, but I met with moderate success and a day later I ate my catch. The fish gave as much pleasure in the eating as they had in the catching. The eating, however, took a great deal less time.

HERE COMES THE JUDGE!

The telling of a story about an event in Ireland is never easy. There are always so many diversifications, tributaries if you like, to the mainstream of the central tale. Nothing is ever simple and straightforward. So it was with the day of the first fish. It really began the day before, so that is where I, too, will begin.

We had been to Crossmolina, "The City" as it was called, and the centre of social life, to book Paddy as our ghillie for the following day. We called him Cross-eyed Paddy to distinguish him from others, of whom there was a considerable number bearing the same name. He was remarkable also for having only one visible tooth, a ferocious expression and several days' growth of stubble on his chin. These latter characteristics were, however, common to 30 or 40 other Paddies. Only our Paddy had the ability to affix you with a steely glare from one eye while the other scanned the lough, watched his boat or followed a pair of pretty legs down the street.

Booking Paddy was not so simple as it sounds. A regular inhabitant of all the many inns he was and, even when one hit off his line, the chase could be a long one. It was no good being in a hurry. "You'll be stopping for a quick one then?" or "Won't you be having a wee tincture with us?" and a story or two to be exchanged at each stopping place. "Did you not see the big salmon the Father caught last Sunday? And him having it in the boat not an hour after celebrating mass. To be sure, the Lord was with him." Eventually Paddy was found ("Well, just a half I'd be enjoying") and arrangements were made for the following day ("Ah, seeing as how it's empty, I wouldn't be minding the other half, thank you very much") and we were able to return to our holiday home.

Arrived at our destination, we were surprised to see a car parked beside the caravan in which we were living at the time. To reach the caravan, parked at the edge of Lough Conn, one left "the tar" a mile or two outside Crossmolina and drove down a long, winding, pot-holed and narrow farm track, through several farm gates and a farmyard, before crossing three fields. It was not, therefore, a centre of great activity and our surprise at finding someone else there was understandable.

The owner of the car turned out to be a charming bank manager from County Sligo. He had found himself unexpectedly with time on his hands as the banks were on strike and had decided on a quick fishing holiday. With him was his friend, a draper from Cork, who had temporarily closed down his business because of a lack of power and lighting. This has been caused by a strike of the Electricity. It would have been churlish not to have asked them in for a drink.

The children were asleep when an hour or so, several drinks and many stories later, we heard shouts outside. We stumbled out into the gathering darkness to perceive, some 40 or 50 yards out on the lough, a figure standing up in a boat, the motor of which had obviously ceased to function. Across the water came a neat description of the man who built the motor followed by a pithy and entirely derogatory history of his ancestry. "Here," said the bank manager, "comes the judge." This was a correct forecast, for the man we towed in with his boat was, indeed, a retired judge who had a house a mile or so down the lough.

The caravan settled a little more heavily at its southern end as the judge squeezed in with the others. The bottle circulated with the stories and the night wore on. There was one brief interlude to replenish stores from the judge's house but finally the bottles and the stories had all dried up. The bank manager, the draper and the judge bade us farewell and we fell thankfully on to our bunks. It was half-past two.

Some time later I was aroused by a shout of "Snoring!" and a well-aimed cushion. "I was not," I exclaimed indignantly and, to prove my point, there came at that moment from underneath the caravan the most appalling noise. It was loud enough to wake even the children who had slept soundly through all the earlier disturbances. My first thought was that our learned friend, who if not actually intoxicated could hardly have qualified to be as sober as a judge, might have decided to spend the remainder of the night beneath us. A further eruption made me realise that no human being could possibly be responsible for such a horribly discordant sound. There was nothing for it but to investigate, while the rest of the family, doubtless with visions of the little people having an orgy not two feet beneath them, pulled the bedclothes higher over their faces.

I do not know who was the more surprised, the corncrake or I. Caught in the bright beam of the torch, beak agape to produce what to another corncrake may well be a very attractive noise, there he stood. Not for long though. With a cry of rage at this disturber of my night's rest, I set about him. I can admit now that there may have been a humorous aspect to the chase that ensued. At the time it was all deadly serious. Pyjamaed, gumbooted and dressing-gown flapping, my quarry was two fields away before I gave up the pursuit, secure in the knowledge that he was unlikely to return to a place where, even to a corncrake's limited intelligence, it must be obvious that his presence was not entirely welcome.

Paddy's arrival, later that morning, was not greeted with the rapture he might have expected. His appearance, stubble a day longer and tooth unbrushed, was hardly one to inspire confidence when he manifested himself at the door of the caravan. Prospects improved somewhat when I remembered that it was my wife, and not I, who had to do the work today. She had yet to catch her first fish and my job was to sit up in the front end keeping the children quiet and perhaps taking them on an exploration in one of the islands in the lough.

Conditions were by no means ideal. An icy wind had whipped up the surface so that little grey waves chased each other across the lough until they came slap, slap, against the side of the boat. Every now and again one, bolder than the rest, would jump over the edge and join the few inches of muddy water already swilling about in the bottom. It was not the best of days on which to be catching one's first fish.

But she kept at it, encouraged by a steady stream of almost unintelligible advice from Paddy. The children and I went off to investigate an island and to look for pirates and treasure. Alas, it seemed there were no pirates, treasure nor even fish to be found that day, for, when we re-embarked, nothing had been hauled aboard.

Then suddenly, all was changed. There was a quick jerk, a dipping line, a flurry of water and cries of "Pull him in! Pull him in!" Excited shouts accompanied the reeling in of the line until there, suspended in mid-air for all to see, was one of the smallest trout ever to be pulled out of the water. It would not have felt out of place in a dish of whitebait and how it had managed to swallow the fly I will never know. Paddy, however, rose quickly to the occasion. "You'll not," he said, "be throwing this one back. Not your first fish." With that he tapped it on the head as he deftly disengaged it from the hook. "And besoides," he exclaimed, "it will be after making you a very foine bookmarker."

TANGLED KNOT *(piscator frustratus)*

The Tangled Knot is a wader and can best be recognised by the way it splashes about in the water making ineffective attempts to catch the fish on which it feeds. The plumage is drab and the legs are green. Similar types are the Fluent Caster, which has much less jerky movements when in search of its prey, and the Common Thrash, which tends to agitate the water and thus scare off the fish.

Voice: The most frequently heard note is a high-pitched *odamanblast.* Also often heard is a series of loud *eeeeeks* while the bird apparently attempts to remove the feathers at the back of its neck.

Habitat: Can be seen in or near most rivers, canals and lakes. The Tangled Knot seems to spend more time on the banks than it does in the water. While on a bank it can be seen pecking away for long periods while other birds are busy catching fish.

C.C.

GREEN-BROLLIED DIPPER *(piscator somnambulus)*

Being the only bird in the world to build its nest upside down (as shown above), the Green-Brollied Dipper can easily be recognised. Furthermore, having built this strange nest, it then sits motionless under the nest for hours on end, apparently hoping to lull its prey into a false sense of security.

Voice: A continuous snoring sound. In the evenings its song is *ushoodavseenthewunthatgottaway.*

Habitat: Most commonly seen on the banks of canals and rivers. Huge flocks foregather at weekends and then spread out along the river banks, each bird building its own nest only a yard or two from the next. Having built the nest, the Dipper then remains in it for the rest of the day at the end of which it retires to its roost, which is usually in a nearby town.

Tight Lines!

In rivers, streams, canals and weirs,
In lakes and lochs, ponds, pools and meres,
From boats and beaches, punts and piers,
With flies and spinners, nets and spears,
In north and southern hemispheres—
He's fished for years and years and years.

But now, increasing age and gout
Have rendered safe from him the trout,
The salmon, grayling, bream and pike,
The tench, roach, rudd, perch, dace and like.
No more his prey the eel and chub—
It's US, the members of his club.

He waves his hands, his fingers twirl,
While demonstrating blood and turle.
For hours and hours we must endure
His endless talk of bait and lure,
Blue Charm, Dunkeld, Marlodge, Jock Scott
And flies whose names I long forgot.

With arms outstretched throughout the day,
He tells of fish that got away
And, after dinner, gaining strength,
Both fish and stories grow in length.
Impervious to our groans and snores,
Just like the Severn—HOW he bores!

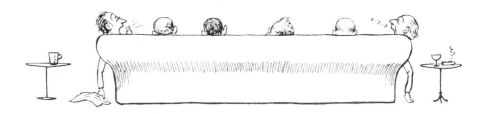

INTO THE VALLEY OF DEATH...

The invitation to take part in a film generated immediate visions of my name up in lights. I could see it all. It would be like one of those epics in which the sadly late John Wayne, as a cavalry officer, sword outstretched, gallops unscathed through a hail of bullets while the villains, well ventilated by forty-fives, fall in disorderly heaps like so many discarded cullenders.

True, my deportment and standard of horsemanship may not be of a quality to inspire others to follow me into the jaws of death, nor, it must be admitted, is Horace's breeding of the sort to make him an obvious choice to play a Champion the Wonder Horse part. No matter, the chance of instant stardom could not be lightly dismissed.

Adroit camera work and expert directorship would doubtless combine to eliminate any evidence of miscasting and we would emerge in a suitably heroic portrayal to leave audiences gasping on the edge of their seats at our dare-devil exploits. Could there, I wondered, be a scene in which, with Horace's help, I rescued a damsel in distress? No, that would be asking too much in this our first starring role, and anyway Horace's back legs probably wouldn't stand up to a double load.

"Yes," I replied, "Horace and I would be delighted to take part in a film."

It had all started when our Master, during a chance visit to a local hostelry, was accosted by a gentleman who asked whether he was, as he had been given to understand, Master of the local pack of hounds. Since the gentleman's appearance was not such as to inspire any confidence that he could be even remotely interested in next season's sporting prospects, the Master's reply was somewhat non-committal.

Eventually it transpired that the inquirer was a film producer desirous of a number of first world war cavalry officers, complete with horses, to appear in a scene which was to be filmed in the market town lying almost in the centre of our hunt country. It would all be done in one day and, yes, there would be suitable remuneration. This last consideration was the deciding factor and the deal was speedily concluded over a glass or two.

With hindsight I can see that I was not, perhaps, an immediate choice, but the request came at a time, during the close season, when not everyone can instantly produce a suitable mount. However, such thoughts did not cloud my mental horizon when the clarion call of duty rang out. Came the appointed day and I reported (at an unearthly hour for a Sunday morning) to the Town Hall, where a large proportion of Yorkshire's population had also foregathered to be made up and dressed in the appropriate period costumes and uniforms.

We emerged, an hour or so later, covered in embarrassment as well as make-up, attired in a weird mixture of ill-fitting uniforms and with our faces for the most part hidden by long, droopy moustaches. Our discomfiture was in no way reduced by the howls of mirth which greeted our appearance from an assortment of friends and relations who had gathered to see the fun. Horace failed to recognise me and shied like a startled mustang when I attempted to mount.

The scene in which we were to take part involved the visit of an official deputation to the town in order to recruit volunteers for the British Expeditionary Force in France. The procession included a Government Minister, the Mayor, and other local dignitaries and, of course, a military band with its escort of cavalry officers mounted on their chargers.

The Master, no doubt fancying himself in the star part, had annexed the place of honour at the head of this motley mob and Horace and I found ourselves relegated to a position immediately to the rear of the band. It required no great stretch of the imagination to appreciate that Horace and I, far from filling the wide screen, would be lucky to appear as anything better than a barely distinguishable blur, occasionally bobbing into sight from behind the big drum. Ah, well, over-night stardom has, I believe, sprung from lesser beginnings.

There was a lot of shuffling about while men with wireless sets and megaphones dashed about. Positioned as we were at the tail-end, the order to advance did not reach us. The first intimation we had that things were under way was a sudden and discordant cacophony of sound emanating from the instrumentalists in front of us. Horace (and who can blame him?) took exception to the manner in which he was awakened from the slumber into which he had fallen and took off into a nearby flowerbed. Only with the greatest difficulty did I remain in the saddle.

An inauspicious start, but worse was to come. As we entered the main street, the well-briefed local residents erupted from their houses, waving and cheering while what seemed like thousands of small children, equipped with Union Jacks, whistles and rattles, ran alongside us adding to the already deafening din. To this, also, Horace demurred, particularly when an ill-mannered urchin applied the point of a flagstick to his not-inconsiderable rear end.

This was just a practice run. At the end of the street we executed an about-turn and returned to our starting place. Again the clash of cymbals and the advance was repeated. By now the wretched ragamuffin with the pointed stick, possibly on the orders of a malicious film director, had decided that a more or less regular posterial prod was to be a feature of the film. This time, however, Horace got his own back, releasing a large quantity of well-digested food on to the roadway in front of the offensive child, who was, I am glad to say, barefoot. Thereafter we were able to proceed unmolested.

Far from that being the final run, it was only the second of many that took us back and forth up and down the street until well past lunchtime. When the time for a break finally came, the cavalry fell in in double-quick order at the bar of the nearest inn where, eschewing the more solid refreshment on offer and pausing only to elevate our moustaches enough to allow the application of a glass, we became what might be described as reasonably well oiled.

The afternoon saw a repeat performance of the morning's activities, the procession parading interminably through different parts of the town. The effects of the liquid luncheon and a steaming hot day began to tell. Make-up ran in rivulets down weary faces and once proud moustachios slid grotesquely down tired chins. The horses, by now inured to anything, were one and all asleep, waking only to snatch a chance carrot from one of the many market stalls.

At one point an eager sound-effects man ran beside me, his boom microphone held close to Horace's feet to record the clip-clop of British cavalry on the move. I had not the heart to tell him that, of all the horses on parade, Horace was the only one without any shoes —

our blacksmith being on holiday at the time. He must have been mystified, when playing it over that night, to hear, instead of the expected clatter, a gentle phut-phutting sound.

The evening session saw us all assembled in the market square for the "Your country needs you" speeches by the aforementioned dignitaries. To our great relief, lined up behind a raised dais, we discovered that my wife and a large basket containing alcoholic refreshment could remain concealed from the cameras behind a huge Union Jack which draped the platform. From this advantageous position she dashed out between scenes with liquid nourishment. Sort of shots between shots, so to speak.

Even so, the day was long and wearisome and it ended with a lengthy haggle over the monetary value of our contribution to the proceedings. The final agreement resulted in Horace being paid exactly twice as much as I was. In spite of the disappointment caused by my realisation that a star would not, at least for the time being, adorn my dressing-room door, I think he deserved every penny of it.

TRIALS AND ERRORS

In the Services one is recruited for a job nobody wants by "I-want-three-volunteers-You-You-and-You". In civilian life it is done rather more subtly. First you hold a meeting at which, by accident or design, the "volunteer" you want is not present.

When the job that needs doing comes up for discussion everyone does their best not to catch the chairman's eye. Then the name of the absent one is mentioned. Immediately those who had sunk down in their chairs rise up with cries of "Jolly good chap, couldn't think of a better." "First-class idea." Feigned surprise "Oh, isn't he here?" Carried nem, as the Romans used to say, con.

I rode up to the Boxing Day meet with a fair sized hangover from the Christmas Day festivities. Separate tourniquets applied to each eye had prevented me from bleeding to death but various well known potions had entirely failed to dislodge a little man with a pneumatic drill who had taken up position athwart my right temple. One of my false teeth was aching quite badly.

At the risk of my head falling apart, I raised my hat to the Master and made a beeline for where the hair of the dog was being served up.

"Morning, Christopher, come and have a word with the Chairman for a moment." Dutifully I wheeled about.

On another day, in another place I might have escaped. As it was I had meekly run up the white flag in less than two minutes. The job of organising the Hunter Trials was mine.

The previous organiser was kind enough to give me some helpful advice on what was required. In no time at all, hazards of different shapes and sizes began to spring up — all of them equally fearsome. Perhaps the job wasn't so bad after all. At least not until I heard of the organiser's two "perks."

It was, apparently, a tradition that the organiser should be the first to attempt the horseborne circumnavigation of the course. To say that my hair turned white would be an exaggeration but there are, without doubt, numbers of grey hairs in my head which I swear were not there before receipt of this horrendous piece of news.

The other jolly perk that went with the job was emptying the elsans at the end of the day. Promises, promises. Empty ones, at that.

During the weeks preceding the day of the Trials, the thud of mallet on post, the tapping of nails, the occasional oath following the tapping of a thumb could be heard about the course. Flags, arrows and signs sprang up in bewildering profusion.

Darkness was falling on the evening before the great day when the final marker post went into the ground. Exhausted with my labours, I should have retired to bed at this point so as to be fresh for the horrors of the next day. However, in a foolish moment I was to regret, I had accepted an invitation to attend the annual Beagle Ball that evening and dinner with the Master before that. Worse still, it was the night for the clocks to go forward, which meant the loss of an hour's sleep.

The night was a good one although I must confess that I am a little hazy about some of the details. For example, I can remember the port decanter coming round for the sixth (or was it the seventh?) time. On the other hand I am at a loss to explain my reasons for being on the outside of the banisters 15ft above the hall floor, though I have it on good authority that I indeed was.

People at the other end of the village have told me that they can clearly hear our alarm clock going off. That morning, in spite of the clock being about a foot away from my ear, I heard it not. The telephone ringing about an hour later did wake my wife, however — otherwise I doubt if I would have made the Trials at all. The reason for the telephone call was complicated. The wife of one of the previous night's party could not wake her husband and would I telephone to see if that would rouse him. I am glad to say it did.

It was thus that I arrived — just in time — on the course, leaving my wife to follow on with my horse. Which, I might add, she did, though not without incident, the trailer at one point becoming detached from the car and wedging itself in a gateway.

Ten o'clock. Time for the off! I clambered into the saddle, popped over a practice jump and rode up to the start. The Master pushed a large whisky into my hand and it went down without touching the sides. The white flag went down and I was away.

Not very far though. Horace didn't fancy the first fence and stopped. Cheers from the starting area. At the second attempt we made it. Sharp right and on to the next, a pole and ditch into the lane and out again over parallel bars. Rattle bang and something fell but we were out and away to the fourth.

The fourth was a stiffish hedge with a drop the other side. My drop came on the near side. At the second refusal Horace stopped a bit quicker than I did and I curved (quite gracefully, I am told) into the thorns. Undeterred by the sight of blood, I leaped aboard once more to collect a third refusal and elimination. At least I established a new course record with a fall, a knock down and four refusals without passing the fourth fence.

Next came the pairs. Now it so happened that my partner in the pairs was the very same person whose wife had been unable to wake him earlier. Moreover, his first round had, if anything, been more disastrous than mine. He had been eliminated at the first. The portents were not good and the portents were absolutely right.

Once again Andrew, my partner, stopped at the first though, surprisingly perhaps, I went over. I turned round to see him carry the fence away at the second attempt and then fall off. We were through! Pausing only for a quick pull at my flask, Andrew remounted and, to shouts of encouragement from a large crowd we charged at the in-and-out over the lane. Up and over. Apart from clanging together in mid-air these obstacles were surmounted successfully but, once again, the fourth was — literally — my downfall.

Three refusals each and a fall by me led to a quick conference as to our future progress. It resulted in a decision to miss out 4, 5 and 6 and we came in at the seventh. Over the parallel bars, down the drop wall, beautifully together over the pheasant coops and then a nicely matched refusal at the tenth.

So we missed out that one and the next, jumped out of the lane, in fine style over the open ditch and thence to the tiger trap. Here, still going well, we appeared once again in view of the by now highly puzzled spectators, the commentator having announced we were eliminated at least twice. To a chorus of hunting horns, holloas and cheers, we swept past down the hill over the burn, jumped the last three and eventually galloped through the finishing line.

What with the falls, a fairly steady intake of restoratives and all the other excitements of the day, the other duty I had to perform quite slipped my mind. I remembered the elsans three days later.

TEAM SPIRIT

"I SAY – 'Are you ready?' ONCE – ARE you ready? – ROW!" The last time I heard that command it issued from a portly, white-flannelled figure who overflowed a most inadequate looking bicycle and atop whose head was perched a pink Leander cap, producing an effect of a mobile, pear-shaped, cream-covered blancmange with strawberry topping. It is not, however, that mental picture which haunts me, rather it is the dreadful sense of foreboding which always filled the moments immediately prior to taking the first stroke. A nightmarish certainty would grow that, whatever the other seven oarsmen were going to do, muggins would either be left immobile or, even worse, catch an enormous crab.

I have heard it said, by one with experience in both fields, that the dread he experienced just before a big rowing race was only equalled by that he felt when lined up for the start of the Grand National. Be that as it may, it was not until I found myself a member of a team ready for the 'off' in a cross-country event that the old familiar feeling hit me once again. I use the expression "found myself a member of a team" advisedly, since no one in their right mind would select me unless, as happened in this case, they were unable to find anyone else.

True, I had taken part, with varying degrees of failure, in a number of hunter trials, but such well justified premonitions as I had had on these occasions were as nothing compared with the doom-laden thoughts with which I approached the starting line with the rest of the team. The first time I had gone solo, I was too ignorant to know what might be in store and the Master's generous offer of a large whisky, quickly accepted, helped allay any qualms. After that performance, which terminated with my retirement in the depths of a thorn hedge comprising the fourth fence, things could only improve — and did. Next time I reached the seventh.

The first stages of being a team member are fine. "We're only going for the fun of it, of course," "Just a bit of a jolly, really," and other remarks designed to imbue the unwilling recruit with confidence are bandied about. Then, gradually, things become more serious. "I see the prizes go down to number six — we might have a chance" starts an icy shiver running down my spine. This is followed by the information that, since there is a prize for the best turned out team, we must perform in full fig. The sight of a top hat, sailing in solitary splendour over the first fence, whatever it may provide in the way of entertainment for the spectators, does absolutely nothing for the self-esteem of its owner. The light-hearted atmosphere of yesterday has already evaporated.

Come viewing day and the situation deteriorates even further. Sheer professionalism takes over as the, to me, bewildering complexities of jumping each obstacle are discussed at length. The number of strides between A and B, a matter I have always left entirely to my horse, are worked out in detail. By the time we reach the sixth fence I am devising a number of ways by which I can withdraw without too much loss of face. "We'll pop this one," says one. Pop? I am more than likely to expire with a loud bang over that one.

Barely able to see over the top of a fearsome hedge from the drop side, I observe that it is preceded by a yawning ditch and sneak off to have a look at its lesser alternative. Faced with an imposing set of unbreakable (and, to my mind, insurmountable) rails, I am informed that it will jump perfectly. Before I have time to mention that it is ME that is meant to do the jumping, I am told that "This is a jolly good course for horses." Indeed? That, surely, is not the point. I am well aware that my horse is fully capable of going round the course. There is little point in his achieving this feat, however, unless I accompany him — an eventuality of which there seems less and less likelihood with every new fence we inspect.

By now, I feel like a condemned pirate, forced to inspect the plank along which he will shortly be made to walk. In spite of my better feelings and my loudly expressed doubts, I am persuaded to remain a member of the team. Even a carefully rehearsed limp and the discovery of a number of previously unmentioned ailments are not allowed to excuse me from what has now become a duty to perform.

A marked increase in the consumption of cigarettes and some sleepless nights mark the passage of time between viewing and actuality until, all too swiftly, the day comes. Urgent preparations leave little time for thought. It is not until, mounted and in the collecting ring that I am seized with the old terror. The butterflies in my tummy loop the loop before dropping dead in an inert mass as I observe a mud-bespattered competitor leading a limping horse back from some disaster on the course.

Then, suddenly, our team is called. My final cigarette tumbles from between shaking fingers, rather, I imagine, as it must from the hand of a man attached to a stake just before the blindfold is put on. All thoughts of our carefully laid plan as to how we were to approach the first fence forgotten, we reach the starting line, only to discover that the previous team has demolished a fence and that there will be a delay. The whole team's nerves are now in shreds but, just before we actually come to blows or one of the horses has time to lash out, the white flag drops, we're off and, much to my surprise, I find myself safely over the first fence.

Details of the next few minutes remain a trifle hazy, my next clear recollection being of passing the finishing line, miraculously still united with my horse. Our event is sponsored by Theakstons, the Masham brewers, and is rightly renowned for the amount of liquid hospitality dispensed during the day. Team spirit was flowing in large quantities when I reached the bar and it was not long before I found myself saying I wouldn't mind going again the next year. Of course, there is always the problem of finding a team that will accept me as a member.

BOOT-TO-BOOT

Stamina, boldness and strong legs — these are the qualities I look for in a good point-to-pointer. Other attributes I like to see are the ability to avoid getting bunched at the start and to cope with any type of going, as well as a good strong head. As to the horses ...

Yes, it is the *racegoers*, as opposed to the *runners*, to whom I refer and, for newcomers to the sport of point-to-pointing, I hope that the following advice may help them to avoid some of the many pitfalls which may mar their enjoyment of what can be a very entertaining day.

For a start, the title 'Point-to-Point' may give the impression that you have a choice of places at which to stand, depending on whether you wish to see the start or the finish. This is not so, the races being run nowadays on a more or less circular basis. Not that spectating is necessarily the main aim of many who attend such meetings — far from it. There are those to whom the races come only as brief interruptions in a day of almost continuous self-indulgence, as they move from the rear end of one well-stocked car to another. For them, a more appropriate title might be 'Boot-to-Boot'.*

Though many courses have now reached a standard little short of the established race tracks, the majority have retained a subtle charm and a special atmosphere which modernization may have dented but not destroyed. Unlike the popular race meetings, the crowd at point-to-points is usually about right — small enough to meet all one's friends, but also of a size sufficient to avoid those to whom one does

---

*If you are American, this should read 'Trunk-to-Trunk'.

not want to speak. Then again, there is room for the children to disappear without them becoming hopelessly lost and the subsequent need for embarrassing loudspeaker announcements.

First, however, there is the need to avoid a false start. The approaches to a point-to-point are, more often than not, extremely rustic, consisting of a farm track which, though perfectly capable of coping with the passage of the occasional tractor, is liable to subside under the onslaught of several hundred cars.

Should the day prove unexpectedly fine, an unexpectedly large number of cars will form a huge queue, the drivers all apparently eager to test their springs out on the deeply rutted track. Those arriving with the intention of seeing the first race will be lucky to see the second. In the event of less clement weather, a queue will still form. This will be caused by the inevitable driver who does not appreciate that heavy use of the accelerator in muddy conditions does not propel a car forwards, but downwards. Any shouted advice will be drowned in the tortured roar of the engine and those who attempt physical aid will be drowned in the fine spray of liquid ooze ejected by the madly spinning wheels.

If you have managed to beat the queue by arriving early, your first hazard will be a number of retainers, the first of whom will extract from you of a sum of money for the privilege of being allowed to wreck your car's suspension. You will be relieved to know that you are allowed a second go for free, on the way out. That is, of course, provided you do not need the services of a tractor, in which case your return trip will prove even more expensive. Experienced hands, having paid their dues to the man on the gate, will then ignore the frantic gestures of those appointed to park the cars in neat rows. Instead, they will park at some spot from which they know they can easily make a getaway at the end of the day.

Careful planning is just as necessary to make the best possible use of the time available and thus obtain the maximum enjoyment from the day's racing. The usual card allows 35 minutes between races, but this may be shortened if, as sometimes happens, the first race is late in starting. Say half-an-hour then, of which the race itself will take up some ten minutes. During the remaining 20 minutes there is a variety of activities which may be carried out:-

1. Looking at the runners in the paddock (at the riders too in the ladies' race).

2. Marking one's card.

3. Picking up a good tip.

4. Studying the bookies' odds.

5. Queueing at the Tote.

6. Having a drink.
7. Talking to friends (if any).
8. Positioning oneself at a good vantage point for the race.

Candidates intending to attempt all eight will deduce by a simple mathematical calculation that there are only 2½ minutes available for each activity – even less if other equally important diversions are to be included. Looking for one's wife, for example. Looking for someone else's, for another. There may also be the exercising of dogs, the searching for children, or even a visit to what are laughingly be described as the facilities. These latter can, with the aid of a pair of field glasses, sometimes be recognised by a sign saying SJN3ꓓ hanging on a piece of sacking about three-quarters of a mile away. If you make the distance, you will know you are in one of the posher ones by the fact that·a divot has been removed to indicate the intended direction of flow. As for the Ladies – I am advised that they should not.

You will have realised by now that it may be necessary to combine two or more of activities 1 - 8 in order to achieve par for the course. An example of how this can be achieved might be "How-nice-to-see-you- both-thanks-I'll-have-a-whisky-how-do-you-do-how-do-you- do-what's-going-to-win-the-next?-thank-you-goodbye", but such an approach may lose one a useful source of information unless carried out with the maximum tact, although it will have disposed of three items in under a minute. Care should also be taken over the frequency with which activity No. 6 is attempted, lest the consequent necessity to visit the SJN3ꓓ further reduces the time available.

I hope I have shown that a visit to a Point-to-Point Meeting should not be undertaken without a considerable amount of forethought and pre-planning. The effort involved will be well rewarded by an enjoyable day at one of the great country sports.

Oh, I almost forgot. Don't forget to leave time to collect your winnings – if any.

STONED CURLEW   *(blotto frequentia)*
The Stoned Curlew is easily identified by its erratic flight and bemused expression. When not in flight, it often appears to have difficulty in remaining on its perch. Also, unlike many birds which can be recognised by a distinctive bar on the wings, the Stoned Curlew usually has its wing on a bar.

A gregarious bird which enjoys itself in large flocks − beware the lone Stoned Curlew.

Voice: A loud and often repeated *maykitalarjwunolboi,* followed quite quickly by *shaymagain* and an occasional *hic.*

Habitat: Although most often seen locally, so to speak, Stoned Curlews are widespread in town and country. It spends much of its time in various trees, such as The Elms, The Old Oak Tree, The Yew Tree and others. Its habitat is often shared with other birds such as the Golden Pheasant, the Black Swan, the Ruddy Duck and the Spread Eagle and also with animals such as the White Hart and even surprisingly, the Fox and Hounds.

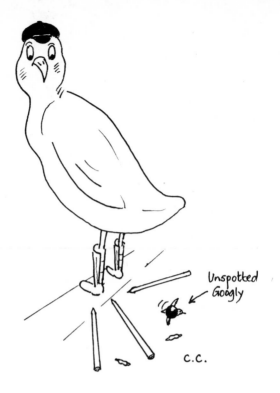

Unspotted Googly

C.C.

WILLOW WAGGLER *(flannelli blanco)*

The Willow Waggler is easily recognisable because of the pure white winter plumage it retains throughout the summer. This makes it very conspicuous against the close cropped grasslands where it feeds. It builds a simple nest of three large and two small pieces of wood, while its mate builds a similar one close by. They then take it in turn to defend the nests against predators such as the Occasional Bouncer, the Fieldthrow and the Unspotted Googly. Huge groups of eager bird-watchers gather to watch the engaging antics of this bird in special sanctuaries set aside for it.

A variant, the Sooty Willow Waggler, is a summer visitor (some have become resident) which has tended to show much more aggression against the Waggler's predators.

Voice: Generally silent, but the occasional call of *kumon* is thought to be the prelude of a mating ritual, as it is the signal for the birds to swap nests.

Habitat: Widespread in towns and country during the summer, the Willow Waggler disappears with the first frosts. Originally native to Britain, the Willow Waggler has now spread as far as Australia where it is known as the Pommie Bustard.

C.C.

PIN-STRIPED COMMUTER   *(urbanicus operandus)*
Male Commuters, seen here about to take flight, have a black head
white collar, grey body and black feet. The female is seldom seen,
remaining in or near the nest during the day. Large, closely packed
flocks of Commuters fly off early in the morning to their feeding
grounds in search of bread, hence it is sometimes called the
Breadwinner. It returns to its nest in the evening.
Voice: On the outward morning flight the Commuter is mostly silent
apart from an occasional *havugotwunakrossoldboi?* On the return flight
it usually makes a steady *zzzzzzzzzzzz.*
Habitat: Resident in the country but feeds in urban areas. The
Commuter's flight lines have changed radically since the beeching axe
was used to chop down much of its habitat.

C.C.

BEARDED PEASANT   *(gaffa garruloso)*
The Bearded Peasant is one of a number of species of ornamental peasants. This picturesque bird is sedentary of habit, sitting almost motionless for long periods, around midday and again in the evening, and has been known to topple off its perch late at night. It preys on the migrant American Gullible and the increasing number of Well-Heeled Tourers there are to be seen in the countryside these days.
Voice: The most frequently heard call is a repeated *oo-aar, oo-aar,* interspersed with *oilavapointobitta-ta.* Its warbling song goes *oivgottabrannukomboinaarvesta.*
Habitat: Resident in the depths of the country, the Bearded Peasant, being entirely dependent on liquid nourishment, can be seen at many watering places where flocks of other birds tend to congregate.

RAG BAG

Telegram sent to our friends Mr and Mrs Andrew Moore on the
occasion of their wedding, which we were unfortunately unable to
attend and which took place on August 12.

WE WISH YOU HAPPINESS AND HEALTH
AND BLESSINGS ON YOUR HOUSE
BUT WHAT A WAY TO SPEND THE TWELFTH
TWO MOORES AND NOT ONE GROUSE

To our Master, who had the misfortune to contract an illness which
did not, happily, have any after effects.

THOUGH HUNTSMEN GET BRUISES FROM FALLS
OVER HEDGES AND DITCHES AND WALLS
FAR WORSE ARE THE BUMPS THAT COME FROM THE MUMPS
THOUGH I HEAR HE'S A SWELL AT HUNT BALLS

An ode to a Cuckoo

Through the whole month of May, we birds sing all day
As we build with a feverish zest.
It's all right for cuckoos and, blimey! just look who's
Laid a dirty great egg in my nest.

Caveat Emptor
(let the buyer beware)

Young man if, perforce, you must purchase a horse,
Then of dealers like Paddy beware.
Of people whose words from the trees can charm birds
Or the cash from your wallet—take care!

I went to his farm and I fell for his charm
When he showed me his 'wonderful horse'.
With his rich Irish brogue this most plausible rogue
Took me in—and I bought it, of course.

"I don't like to brag, but he jumps like a stag
Over timber and hedges and water.
I am sure he will do as a hunter for you
And gentle enough for your daughter.

"D'ye want him for racing? He's bred right for 'chasing,
Both his dam and his sire won a lot.
He has a full brother—belongs to me mother—
Who won ten point-to-points on the trot.

"He's as safe in a box as the gold in Fort Knox
And he goes like a bomb with the hounds.
He is easy to clip. He's an absolute snip
At a thousand—that's guineas not pounds.

"A child could be doing his grooming and shoeing,
In the ring you should see his clear rounds.
He's a horse you will bless, so I couldn't take less
Than nine hundred Come now, I'll take pounds.

"He's only just eight and well up to the weight
And at dressage he really astounds.
He's a real good goer, I couldn't go lower
Than eight hundred. For cash I'll take pounds.

"At showing he's grand. Just you look at him stand,
In good points you can see he abounds.
Ah sure, sir, as buyer you will have to go higher
Than five hundred and twenty-five pounds.

"He always goes well and as sound as a bell.
What? You think that this looks like a spavin?
Ah no. Not at all—just a little wind gall—
'Tis a wonderful horse you'll be havin'.

"All right, I'll say seven. As God's in His heaven.
You can have him at that price because
You're the man for the horse. Sir, your gain is my loss."
So at last I said: "DONE"—and I was.

And that is the reason I lost a whole season
As well as a few hundred smackers.
And I'm filled with remorse that the worth of that horse
Was eighteen pounds ten at the knackers.

Take warning, my son, or you too will be done
If you don't see the point of this tale.
Beware of the blarney of Paddy O'Mahoney
And of others with horses for sale.

Trials and

Tribulations

We've driven for miles to the pony club trials
With their usual ghastly frustrations
And, as likely as not, it will all be for what?
Just two more e-liminations.

When our daughter went first, we both feared the worst—
And how justified were all our fears—
For, just as I reckoned, she stopped at the second
And promptly dissolved into tears.

She baulked at the third and used a rude word,
Which was new to the judge (so he said),
And then at the fourth, when the pony took off,
She fell in the ditch on her head.

She got on again and grinned through the pain,
As she flew over five, six and seven,
But, turning too late, she never saw eight
And galloped straight on to eleven.

All over the ground the ponies rush round
Under children of varying abilities.
And the standard of food?—Well it's, frankly, not good—
On a par with the toilet facilities.

"Get on with it, child!" shouts a father, quite wild,
And a mother comes galloping through.
As they run round the course, their voices all hoarse,
You would think they had entered it too.

"Now son, are you ready? Then just take it steady,
You're next to go after the grey."
Oh! I say, what hard luck! Just a kick and a buck
And he's off, but in quite the wrong way.

He's quick to remount and the fall doesn't count,
He's away—and the family cheers.
But, alas, at the double he got into trouble
And the only hope now is the pairs.

When they set off again it had started to rain
And they came back all covered in mud.
They'd got caught together and broken a leather
And a fetlock was streaming with blood.

When you think of the sweat (and we're not back home yet)
And the tears and the rage and the sorrow.
Though it's meant to be fun, I, for one, am quite done
And, my God! There's another tomorrow!

A Terrierble Day

Before I took Joe to the Terrier Show
I gave him a much needed bath.
Then, forgetting the need for a collar and lead,
I gave him a walk down the path.

He was off in a flash and at once made a dash
Through the gate and, avoiding recapture,
Proceeded to roll in a very dead mole
With a look on his face of sheer rapture.

Because of the smell, I didn't feel well
In the car. Joe was out in a tick
And started a fight with a dog twice his height
Whose owner joined in with a stick.

This caused a furore and, amidst the uproar,
In less time than it takes in the telling,
The rest had joined in with a terrible din
And their owners all beating and yelling.

At the end of the fight, the ground was a sight,
Bits of debris all over the grass.
A trouser leg here, an ear or two there
When they called: "Can we have the first class?"

Joe just wouldn't budge in front of the judge
Who said, impolitely, "I beg,
Would you please take that thing at once from the ring!"
Joe at once bit him hard on the leg.

The troubles I'd had were not nearly so bad
As the trouble Joe got into next.
He spotted a bitch that he fancied and which
... Well, its owner was really quite vexed.

Though Joe can run fast, in his race he was last.
At the start he decided to catch
A large flea in his ear while he sat on his rear,
So he literally started from scratch.

It was no great surprise when I heard that a prize
Had been snatched from the prize-giving table.
So I called it a day and with Joe crept away
Just as quietly as I was able.

I was thankful to go from that Terrier Show
And thus was an awful day ended.
The missing rosette? It was clear who had ate it
When Joe passed a 'Highly Commended'.

They're

When I go to the Races—flat, hurdle or 'chases,
There is plenty of helpful advice
On which horse to back and, though there's no lack,
It doesn't come cheap at the price.

The man on the gate says, "Back number eight
In the first, for I swear it can't fail."
But it's money ill-spent, for the pace that it went
Was that of an elderly snail.

When it came to the second, a trainer friend reckoned,
"My hurdler, it cannot be beat'"
He might have been right if, at the last flight,
It had managed to stay on its feet.

From an owner I heard that his horse in the third
Was just right and was bound to go close.
But his horse was deformed and he'd been misinformed,
Unless someone had slipped it a dose.

Off!

Then a jockey I know said, "This one will go.
It will win—get your money on fast."
Going better than most, it was first past the post
But its rider, on foot, finished last.

And then I met Nancy who told me her fancy
Had scored with a ten-to-one win.
My choice wasn't there and it's no help to hear
She chose hers with the help of a pin.

My next choice was good, for it gamely withstood
Every challenge and went fit to bust.
But, alas, it was pipped and, thoroughly gypped,
I tore up my slips in disgust.

And then an objection advanced my selection
To first. But to my dismay,
Though I searched all the ground in the bar and around,
Every piece had been blown away.

And that's why you see foolish fellows like me,
Who put money on other men's choices,
Walking round without shirts (which we've lost on dead certs)
While bookies drive round in Rolls Royces.

IN CONCLUSION, or, if you have opened this book at the back, as an INTRODUCTION, I would like to pay tribute to Dr. Wuntz, the well-known ornithologist, who gave his name to the bird he discovered. He has kindly allowed me to reproduce here the only picture ever taken of the bird which, so far as is known, has never been seen again.

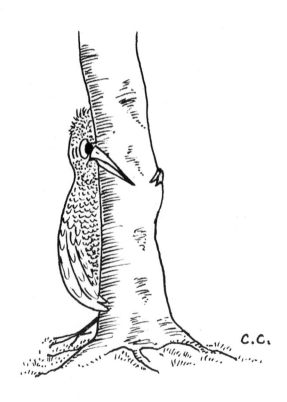

WUNTZ BITTERN – a very shy bird